Charlotte Middleton

Charlie and Robocat

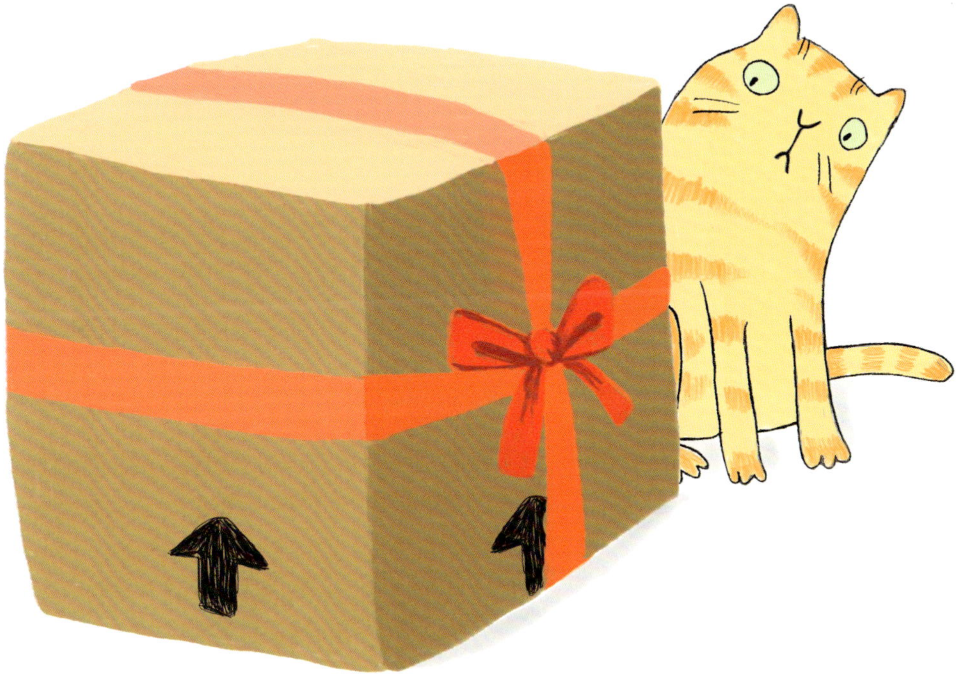

Collins

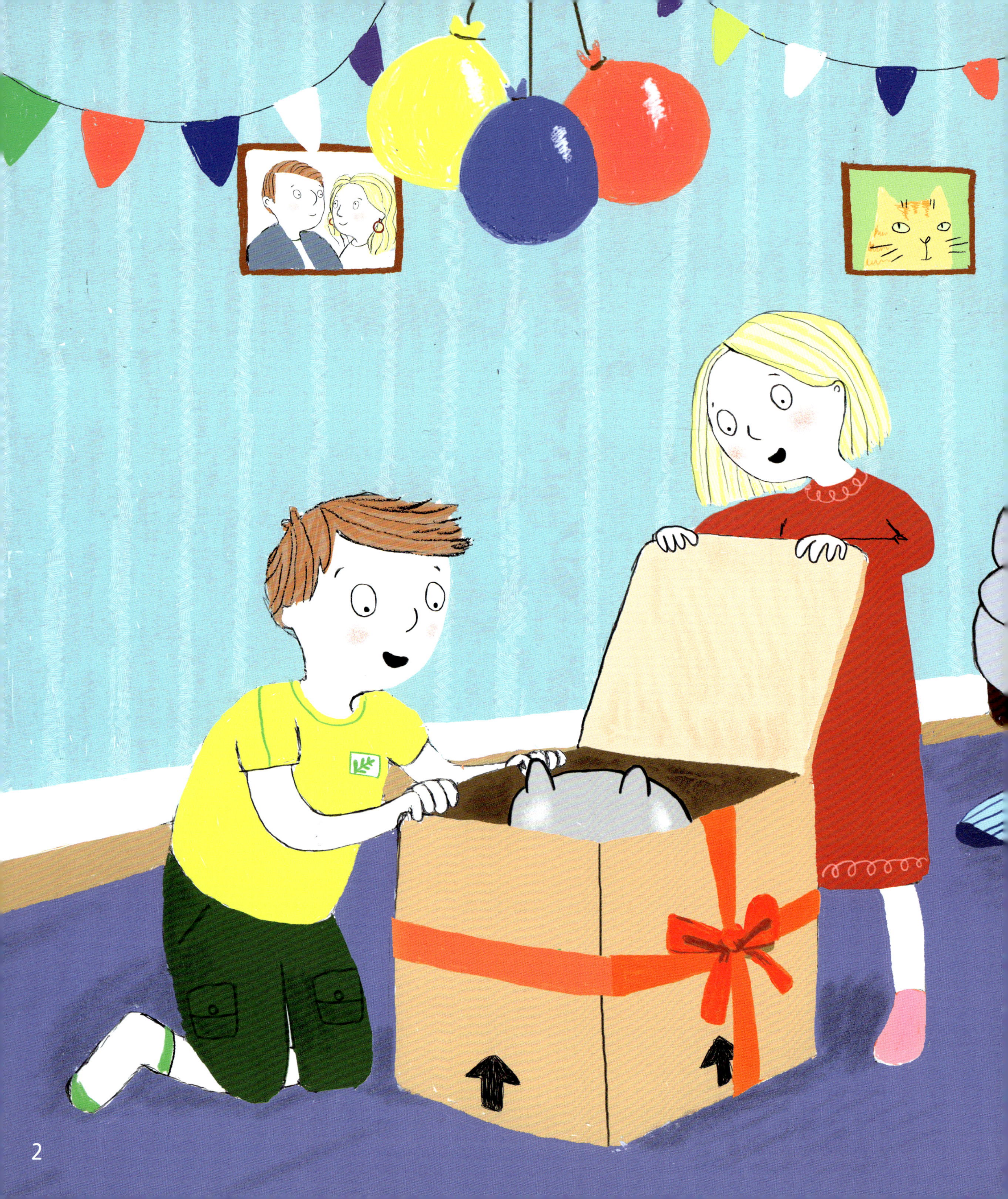

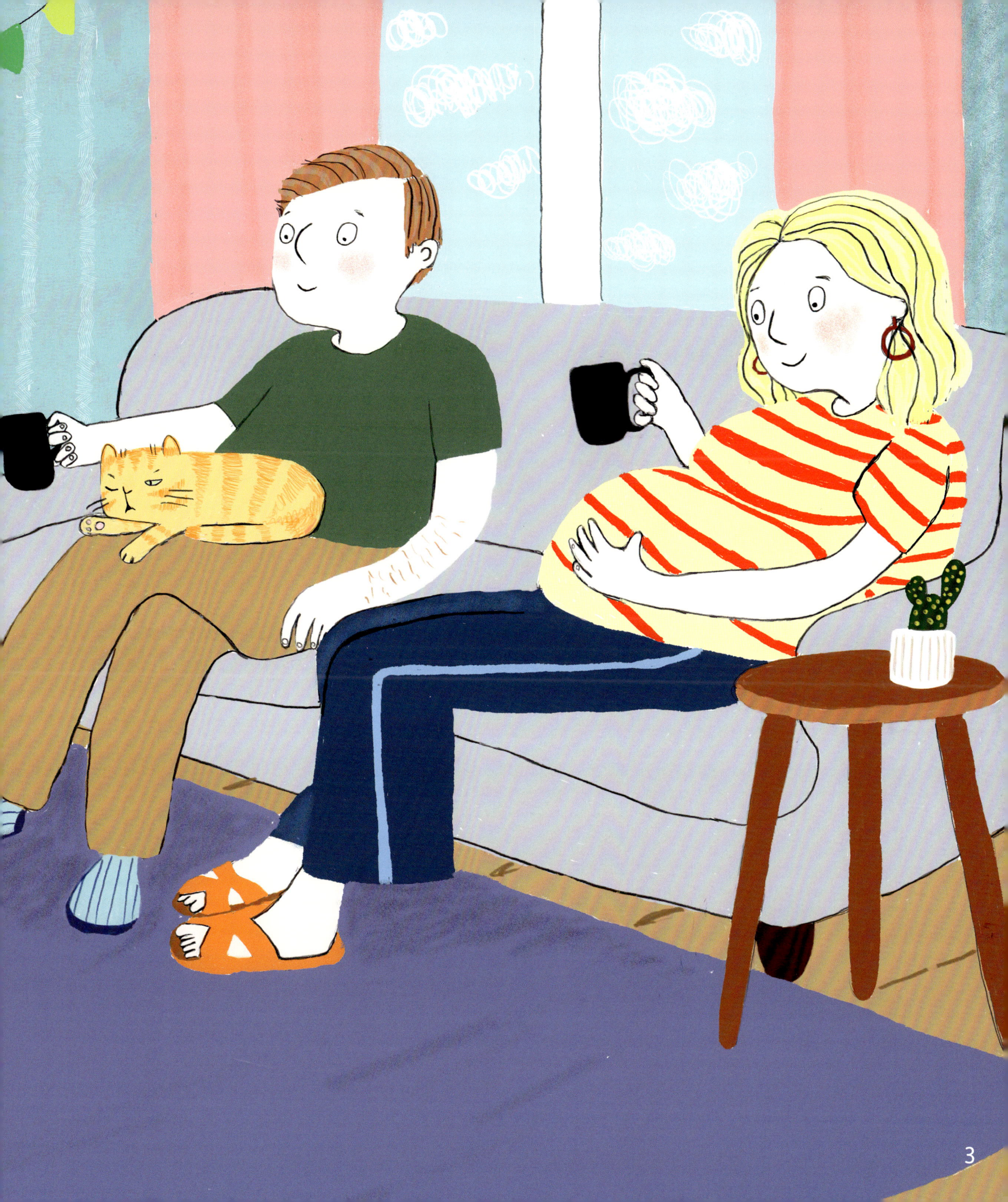

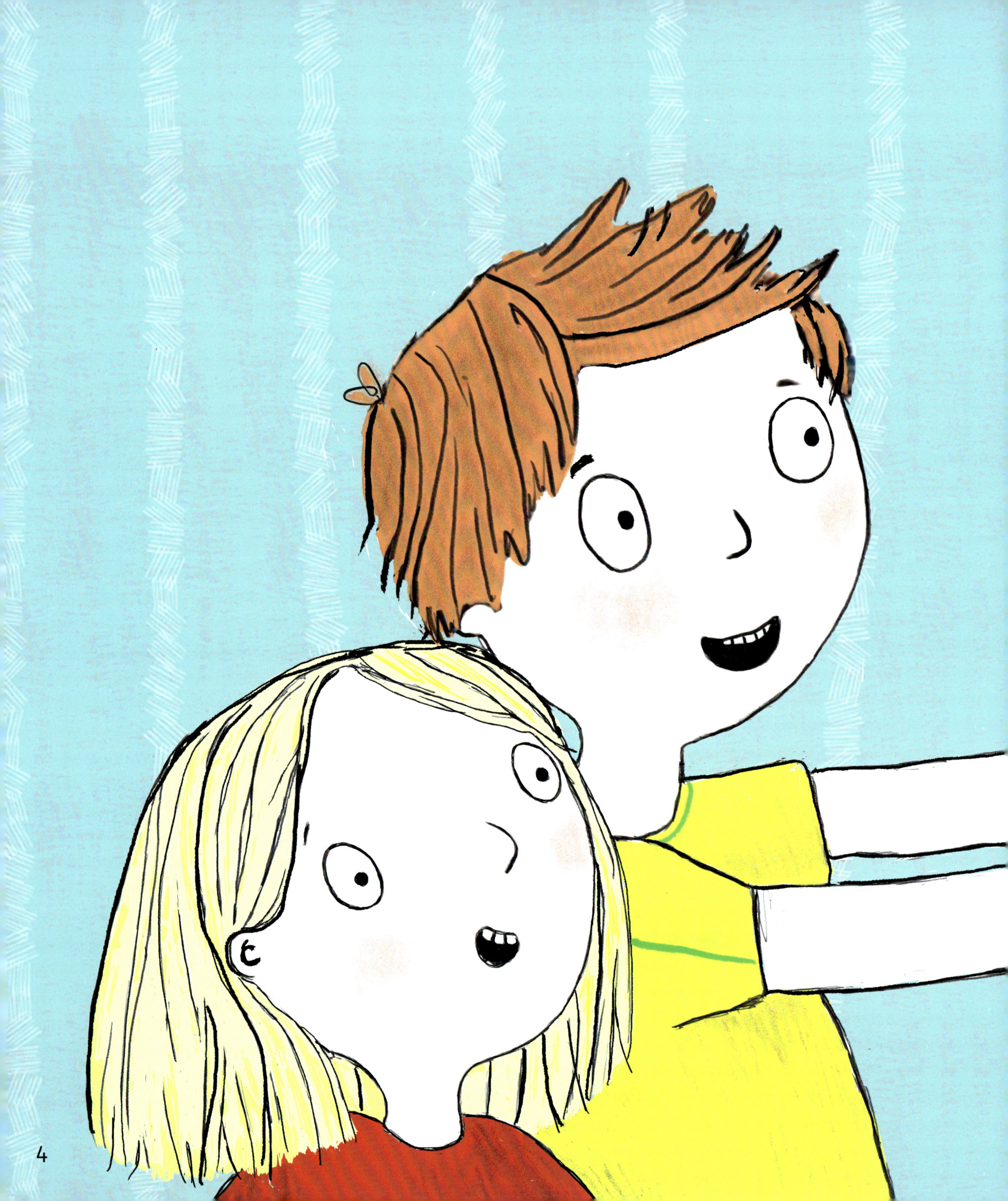

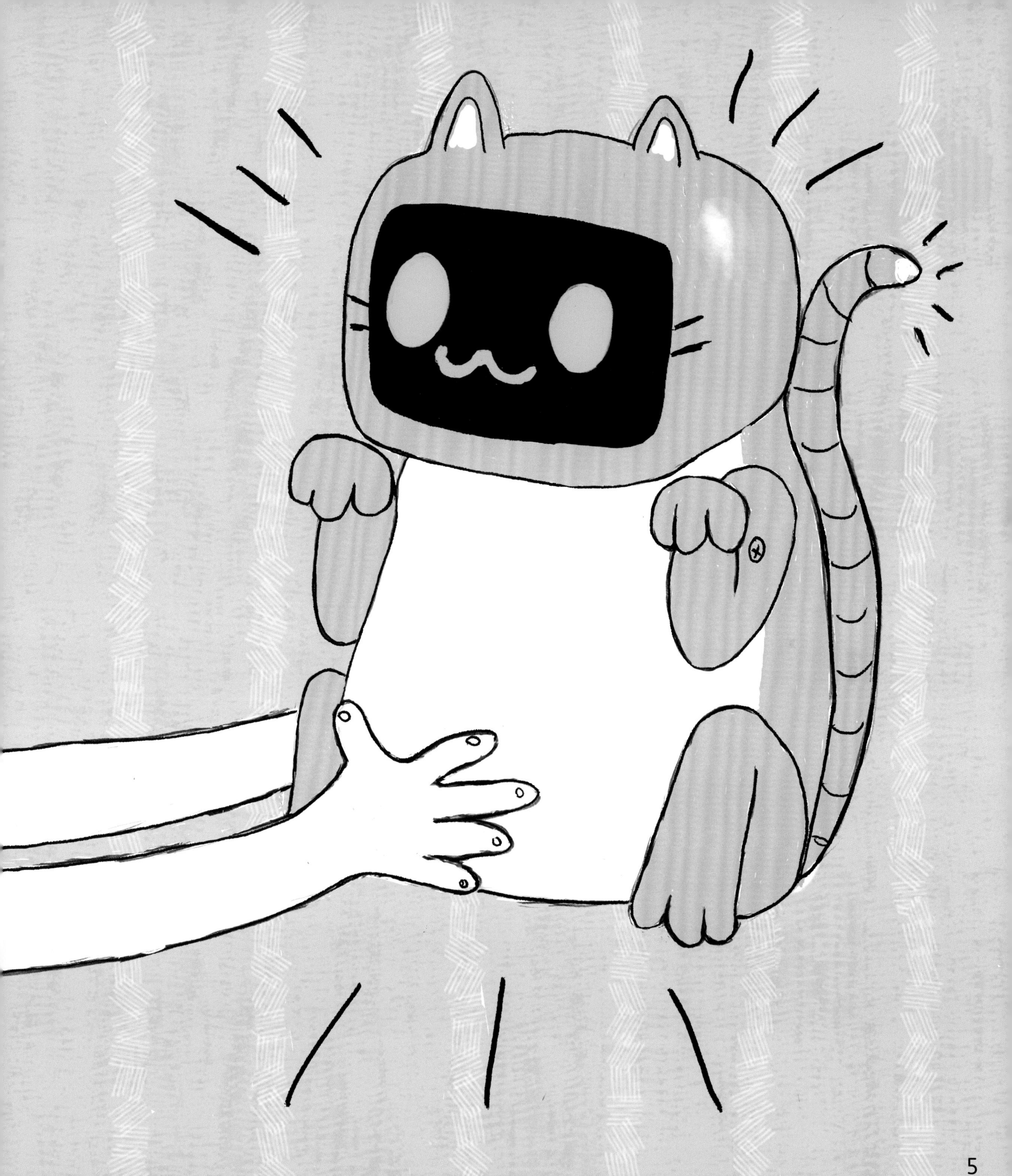

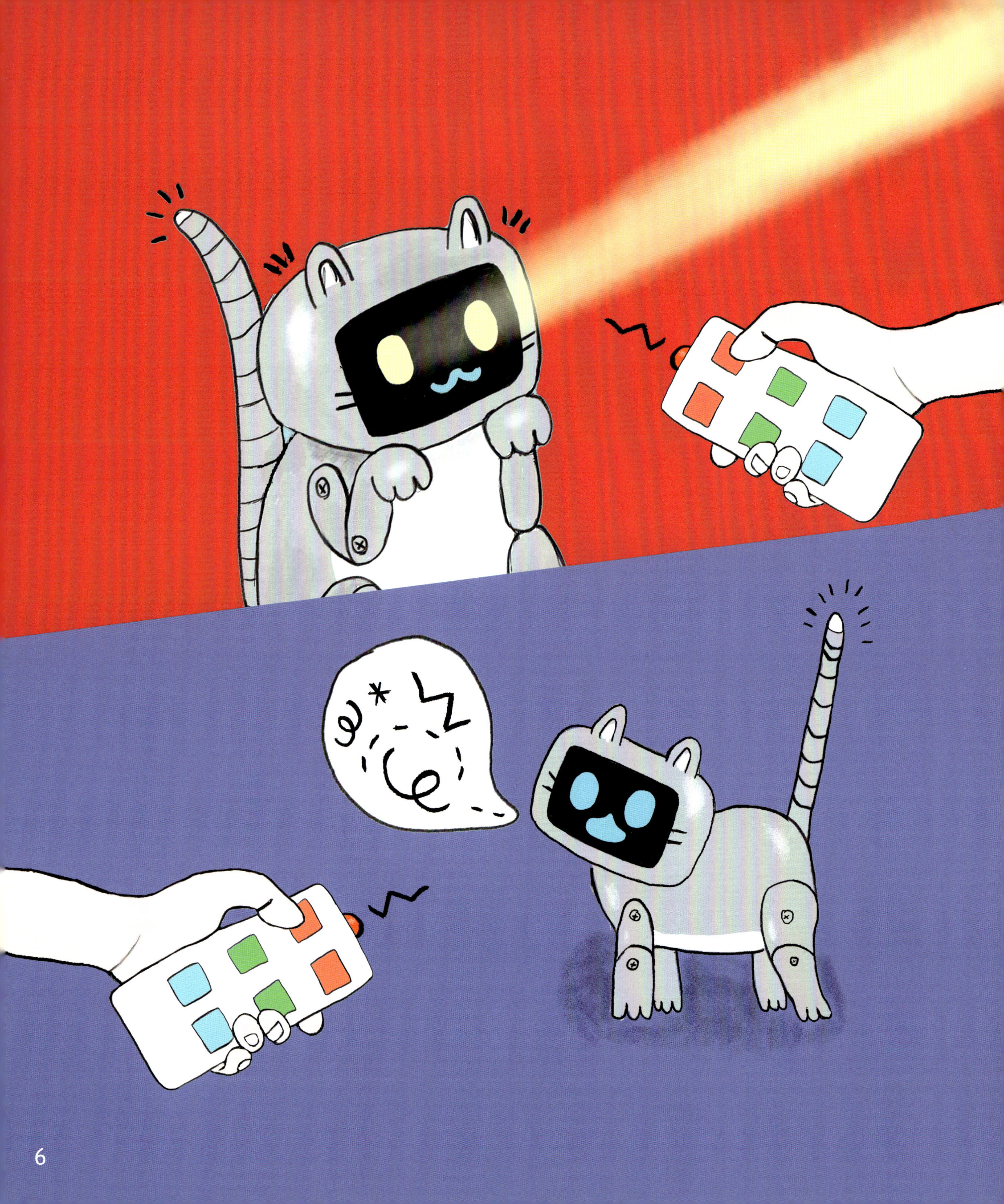

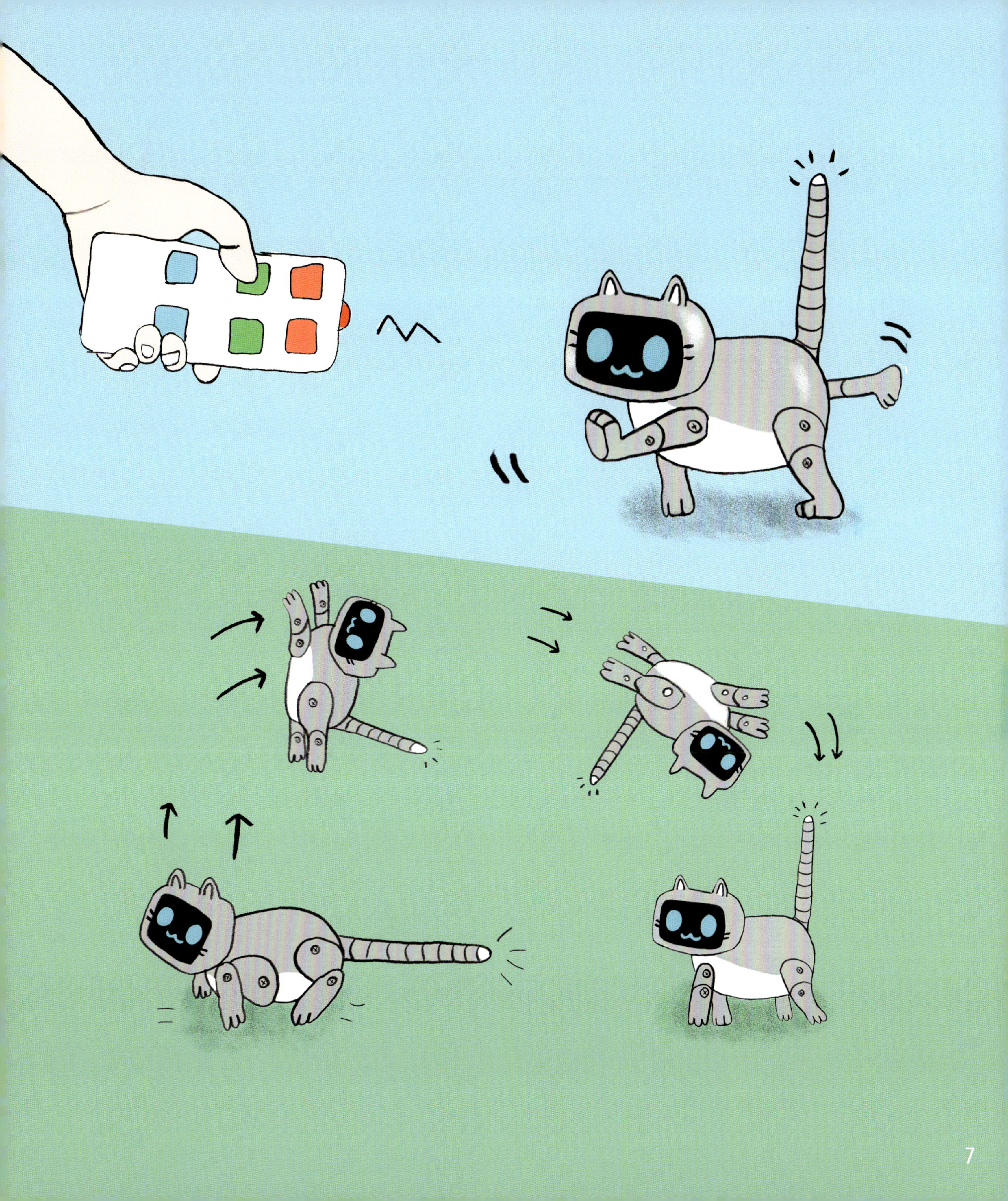

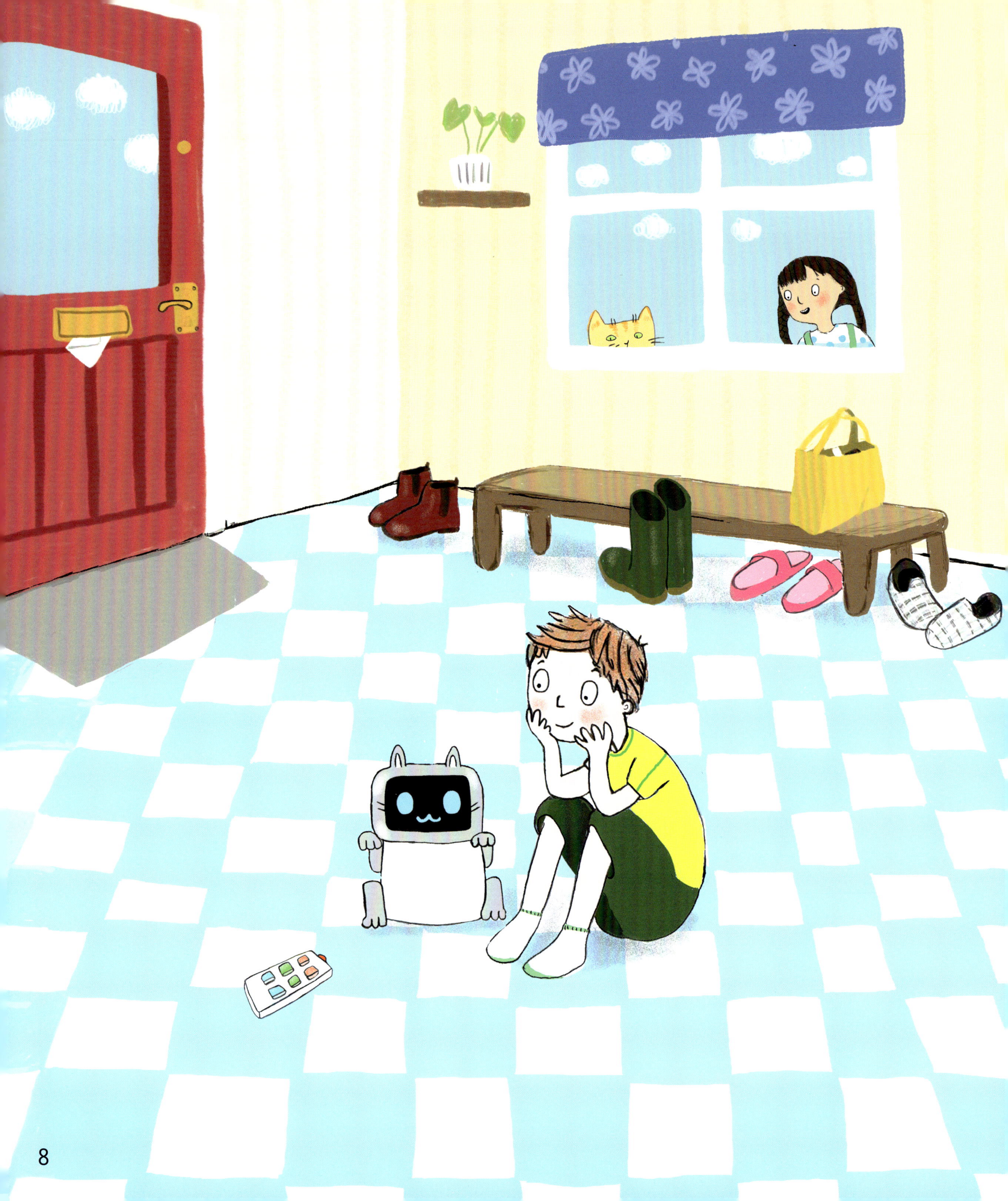

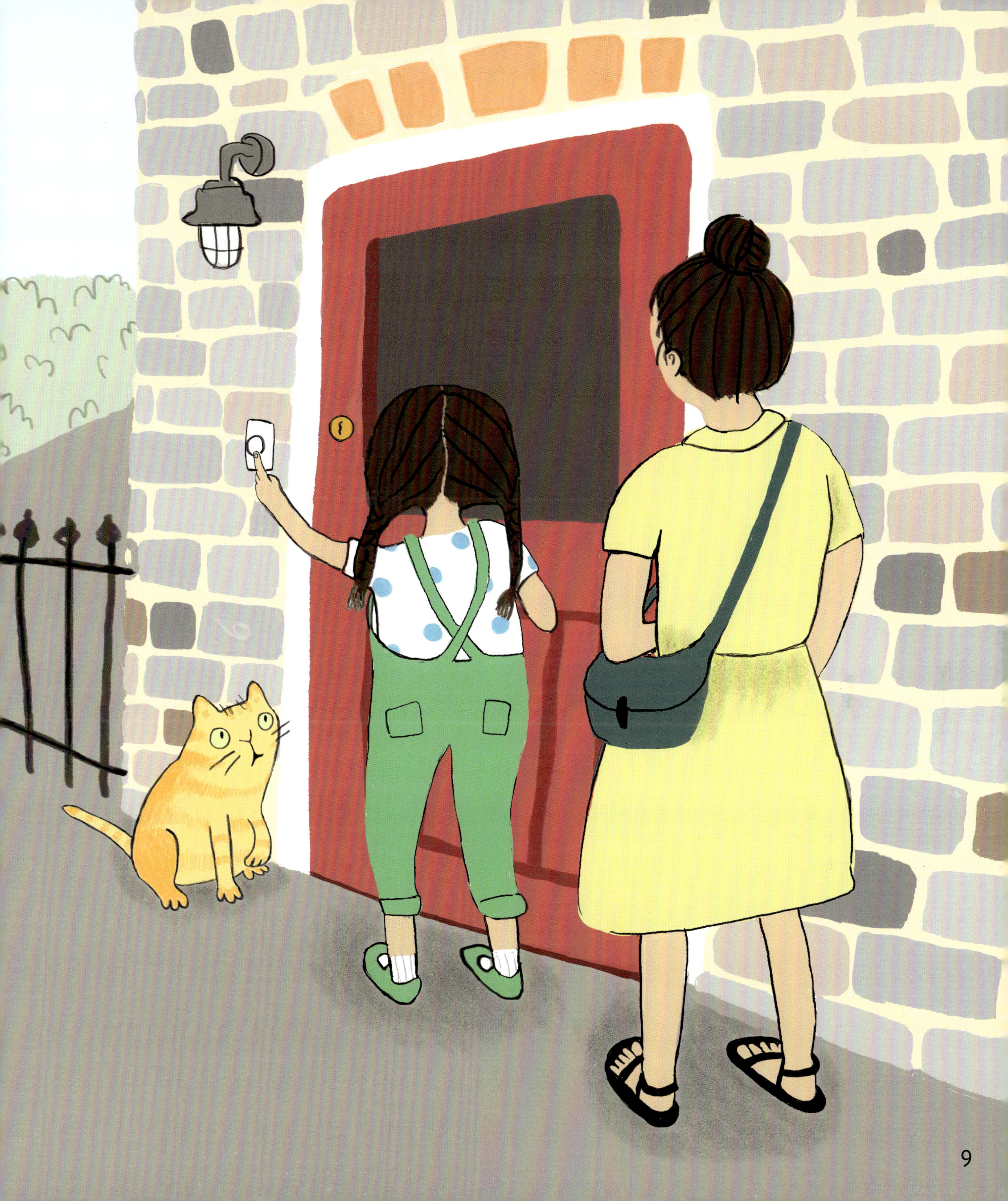

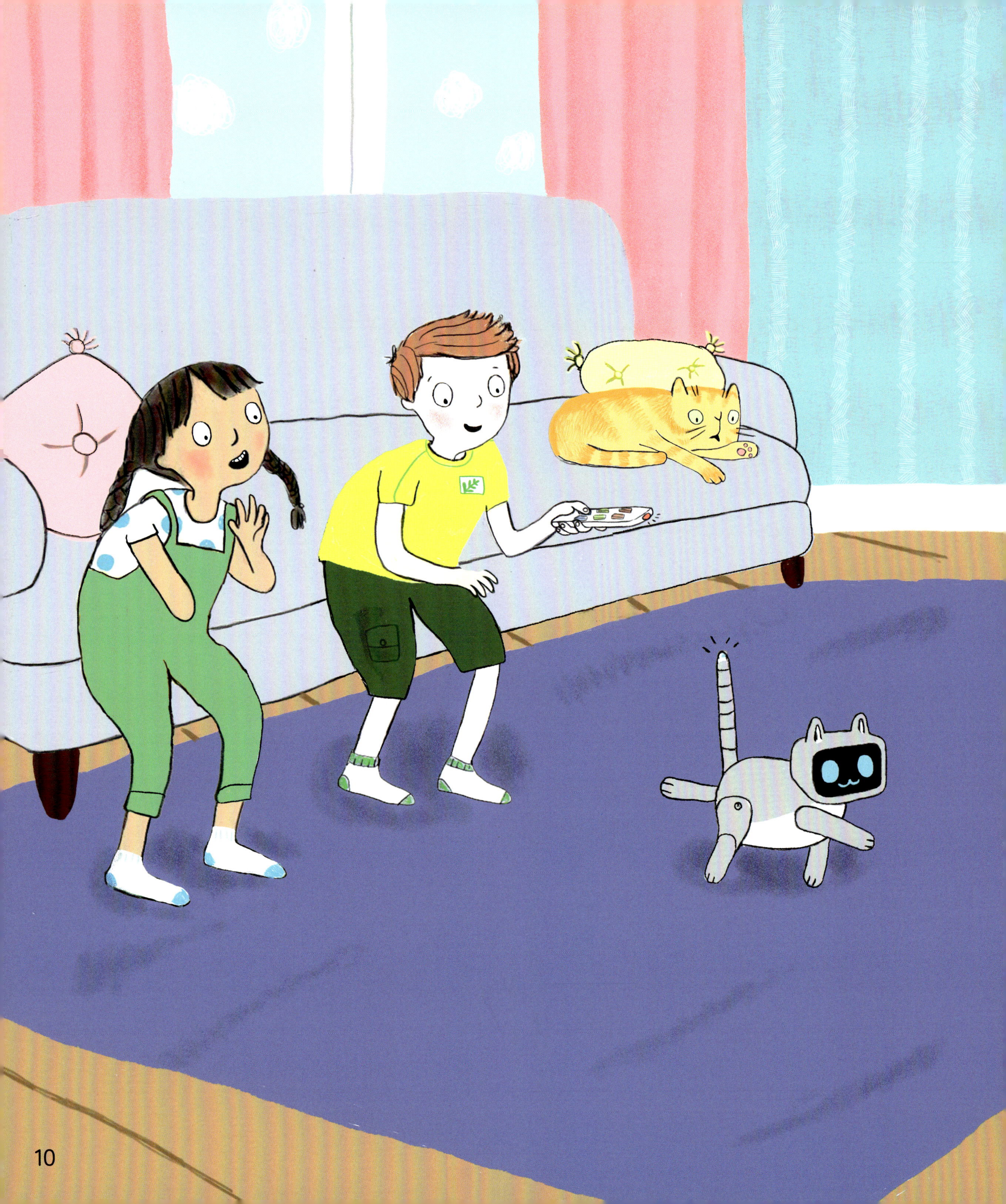

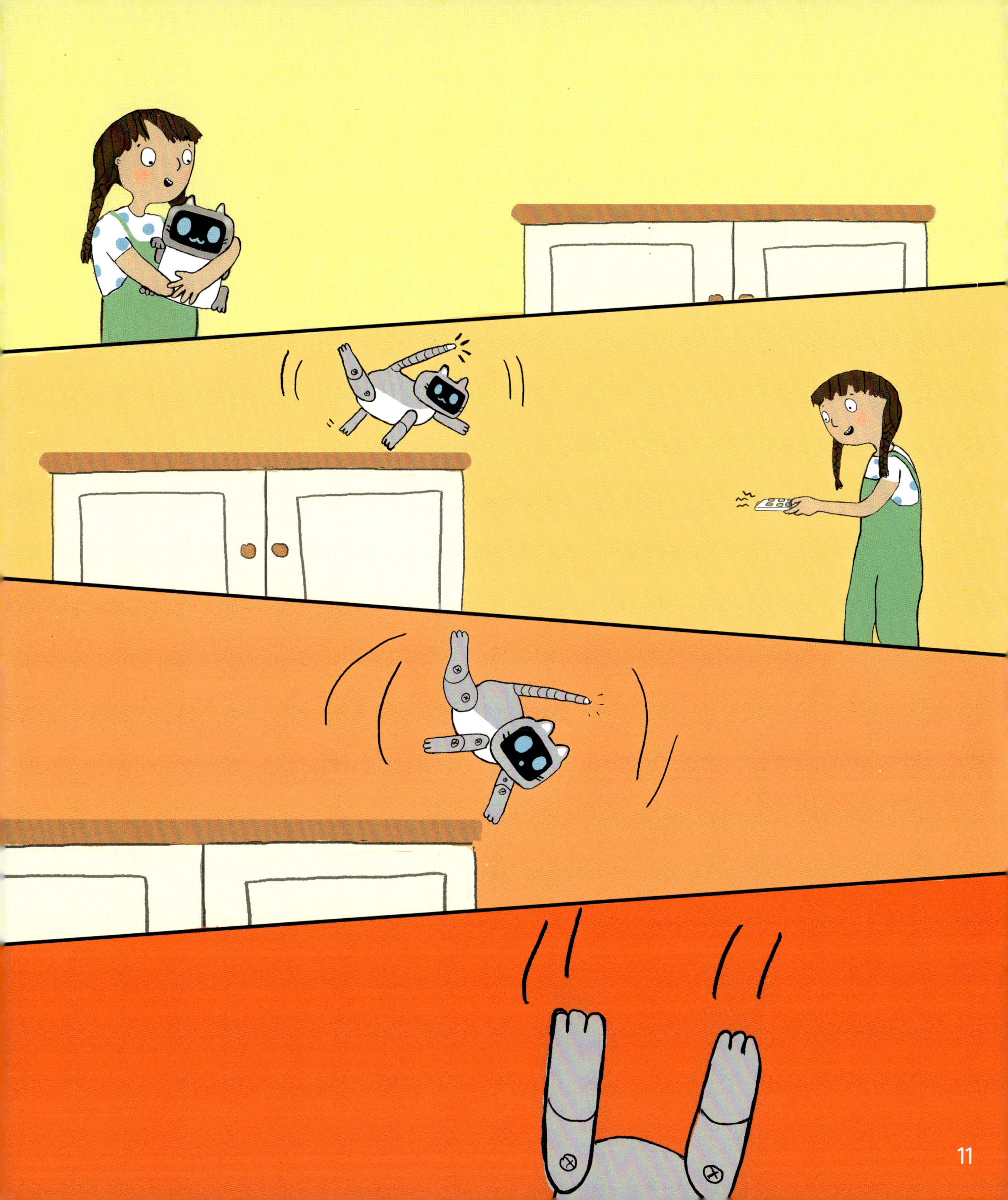

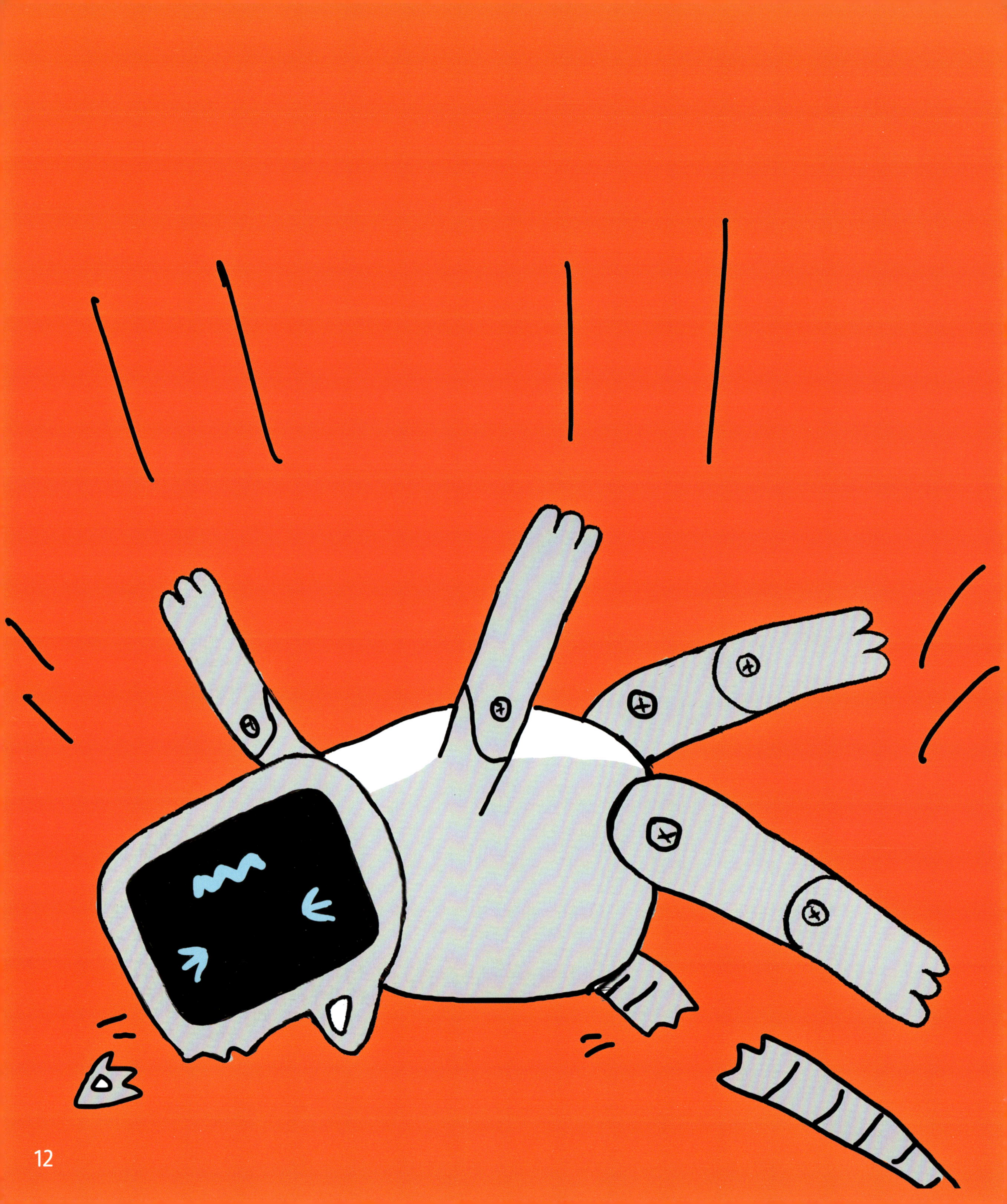

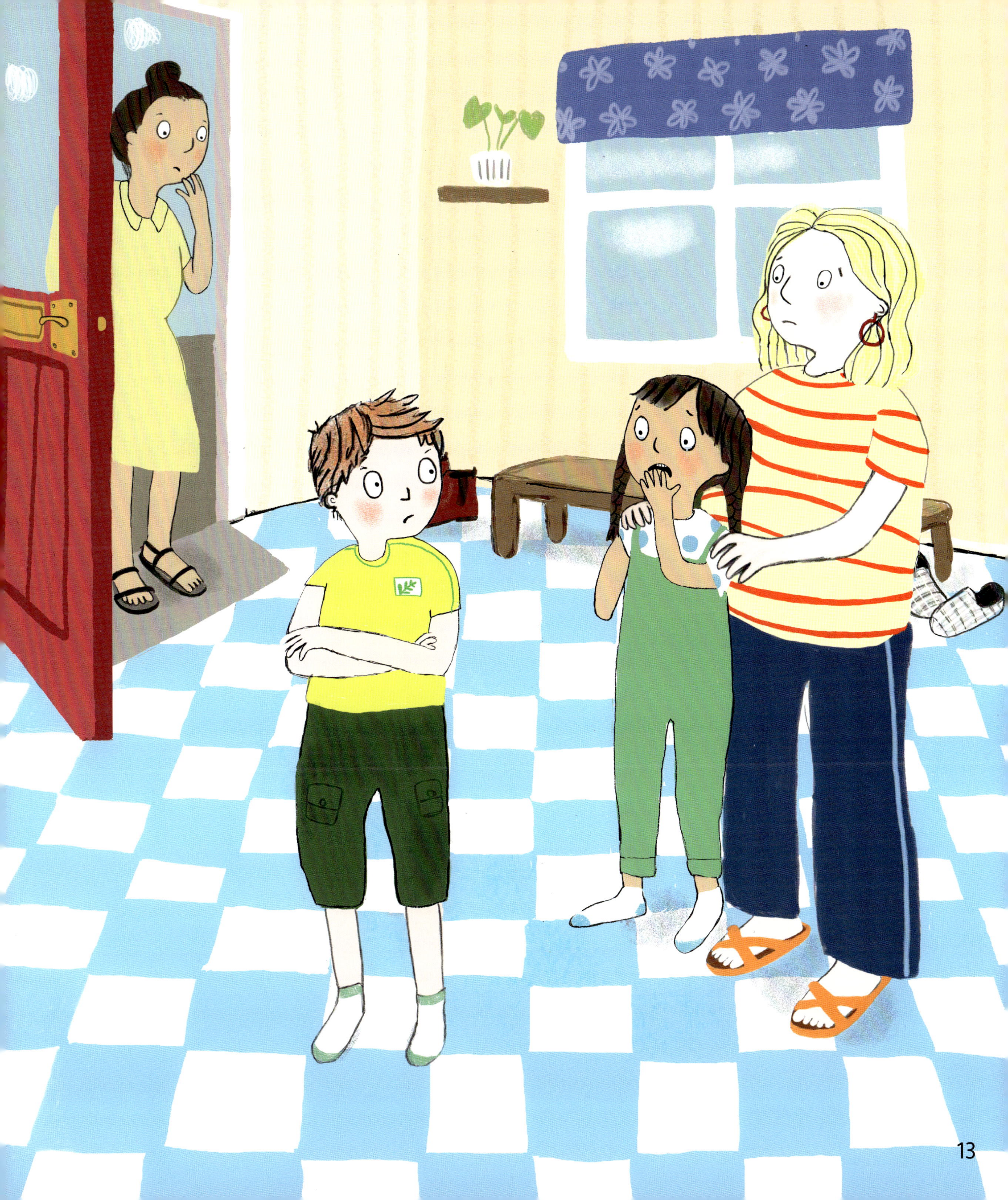

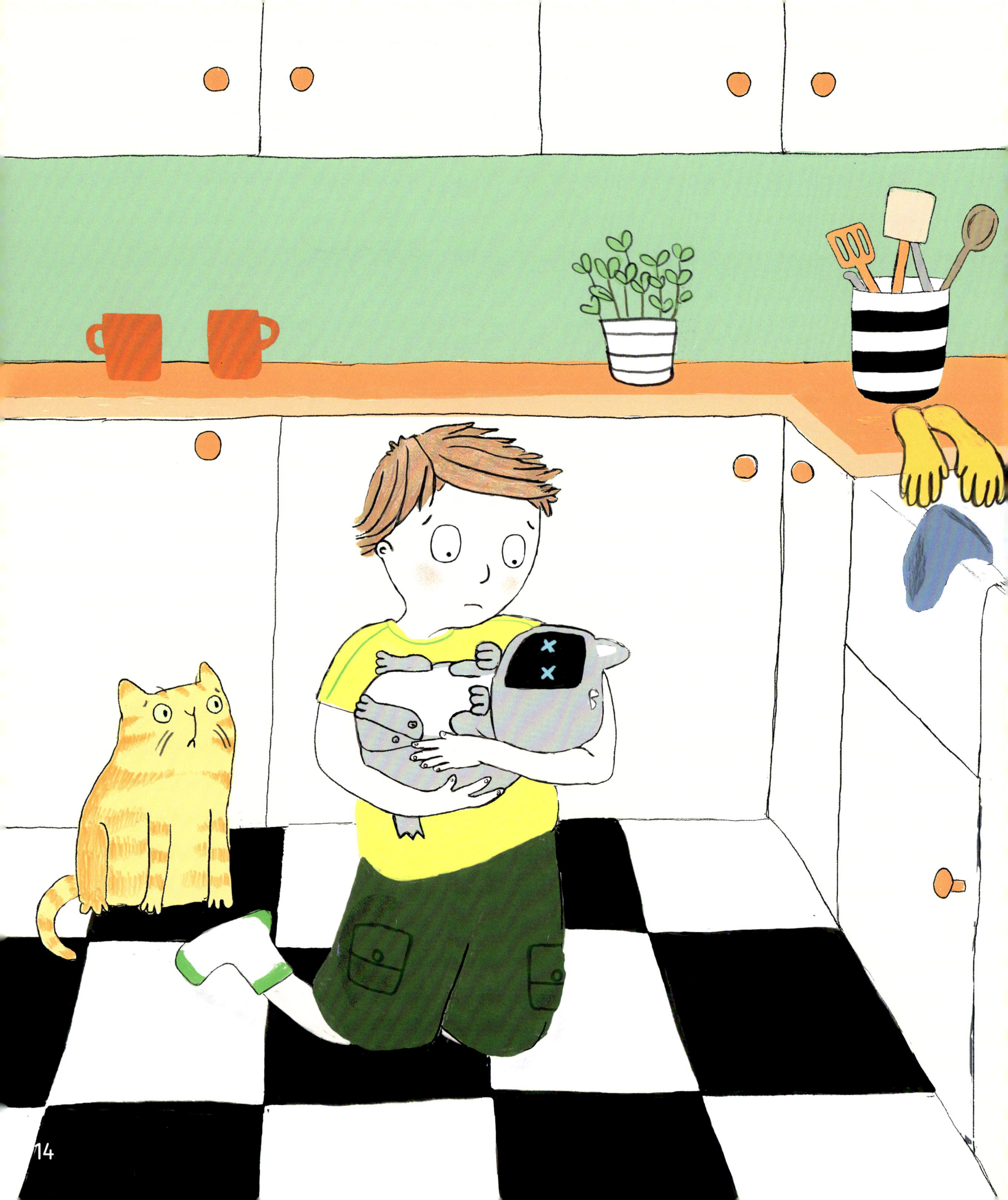

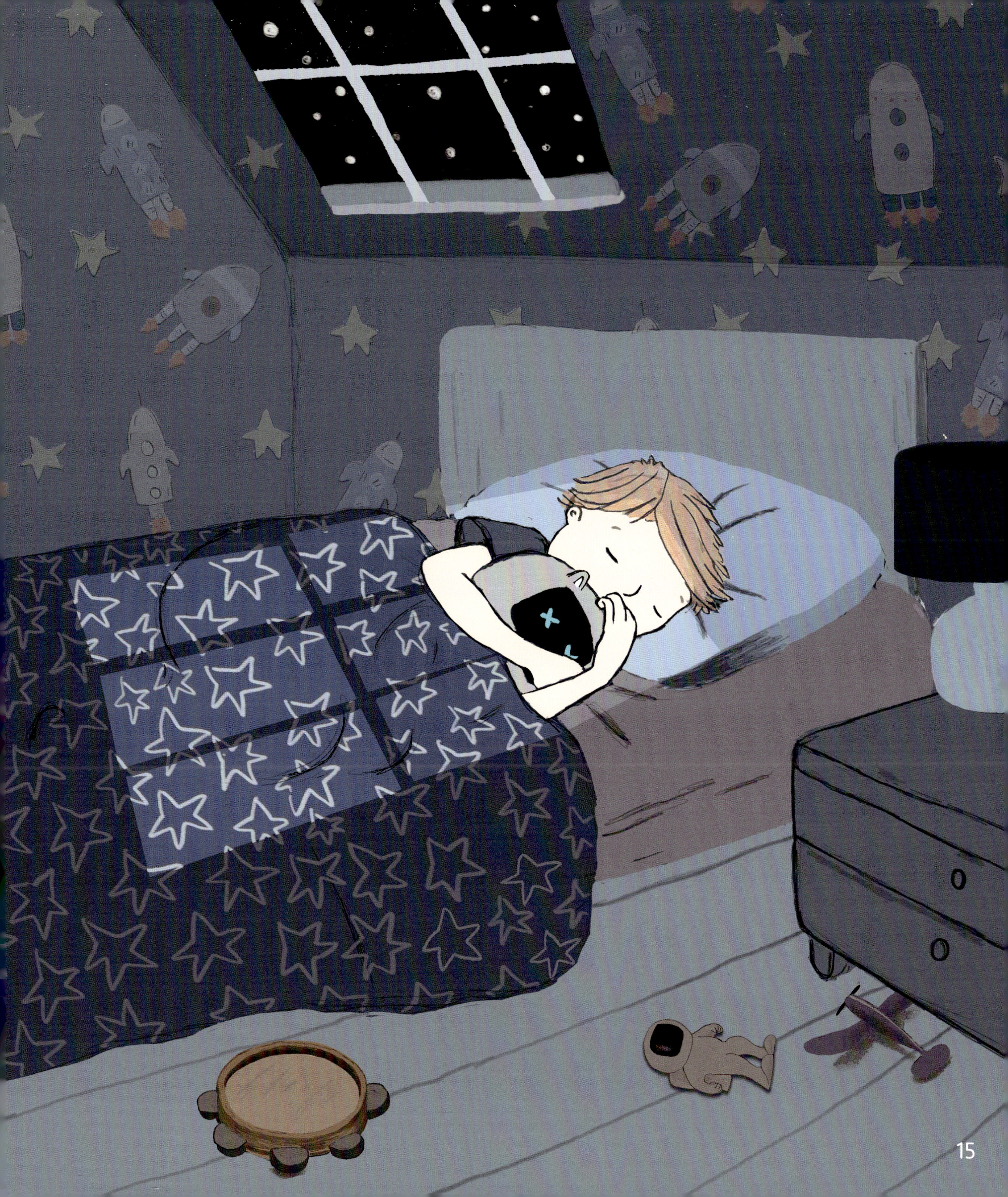

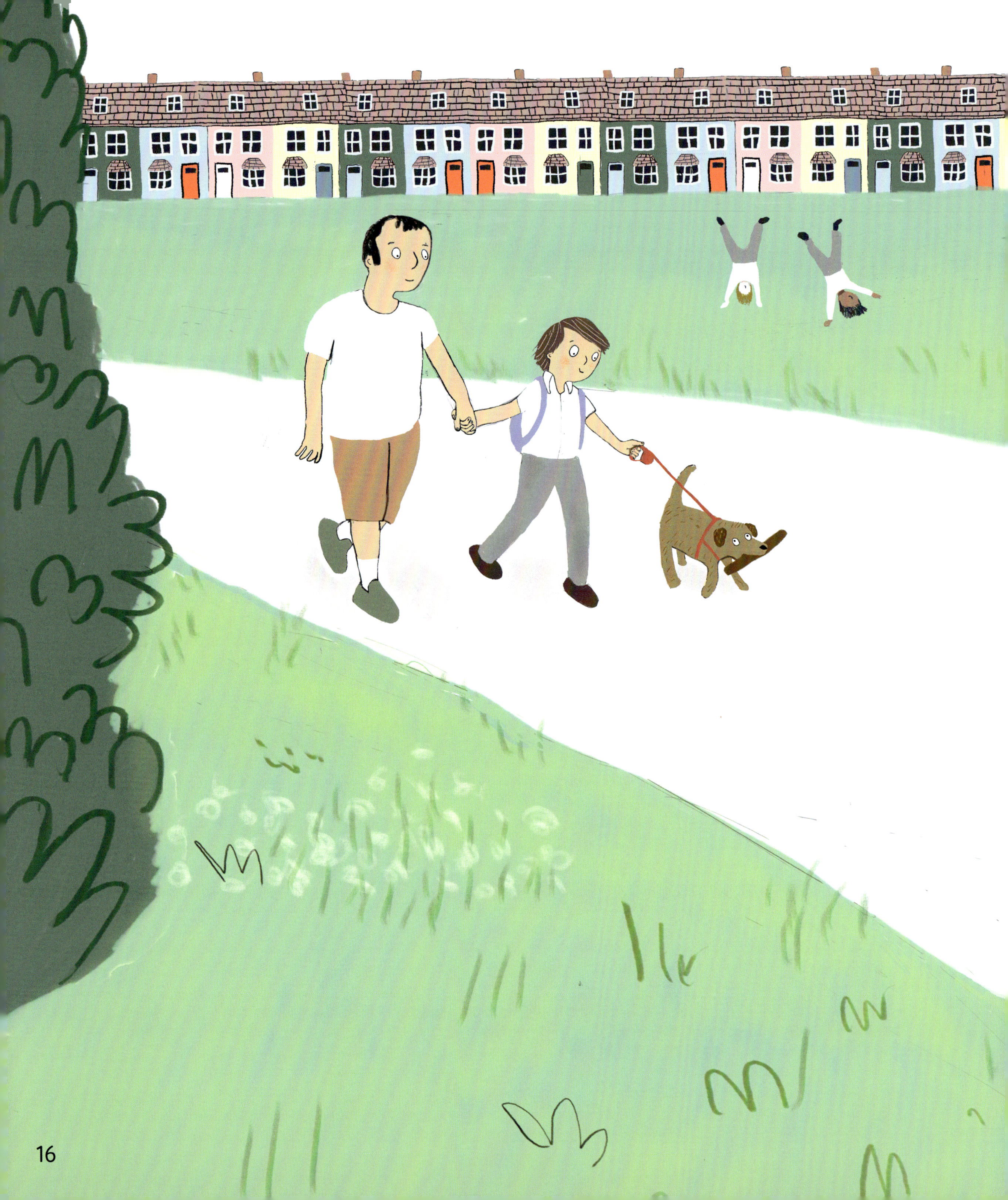

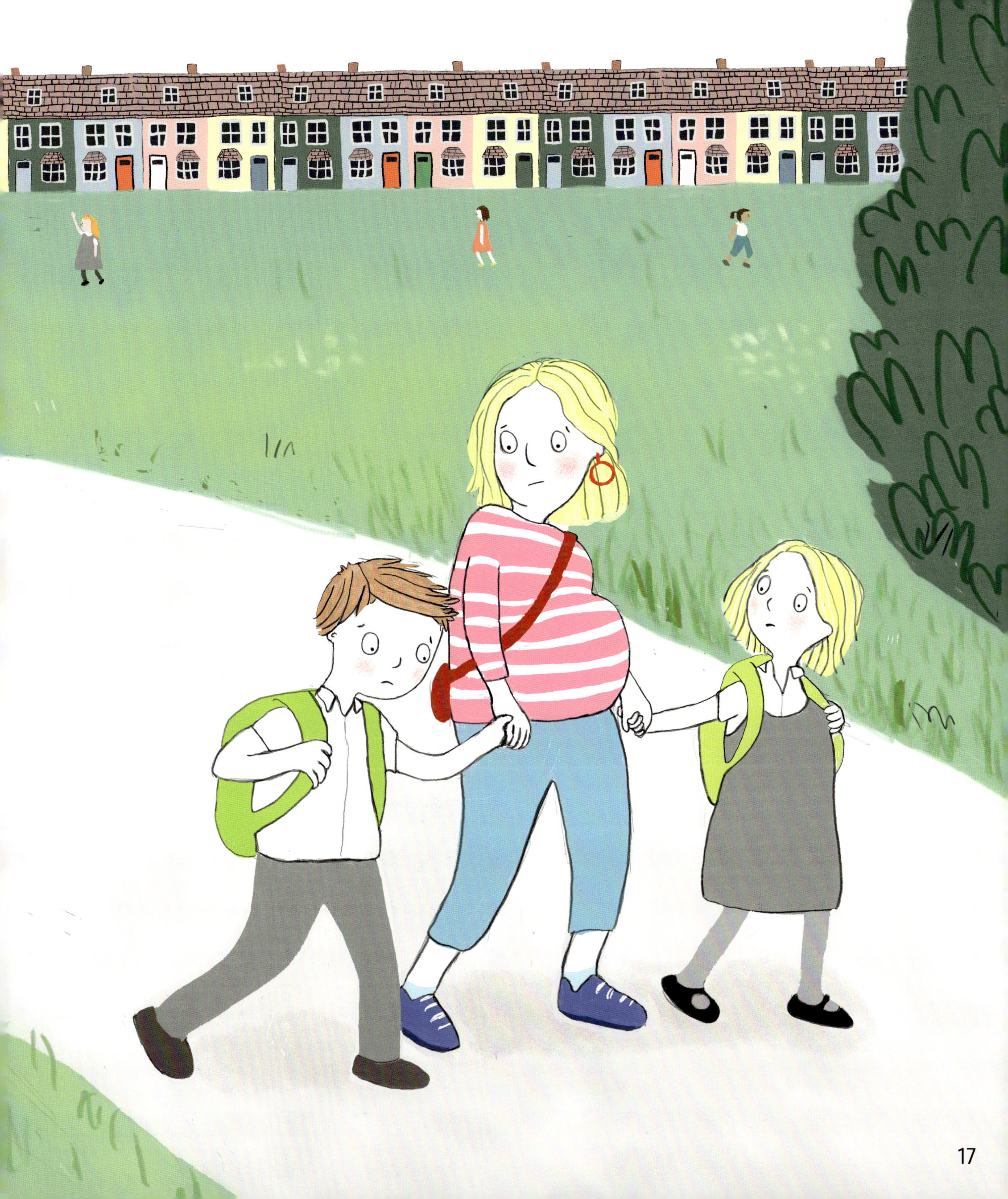

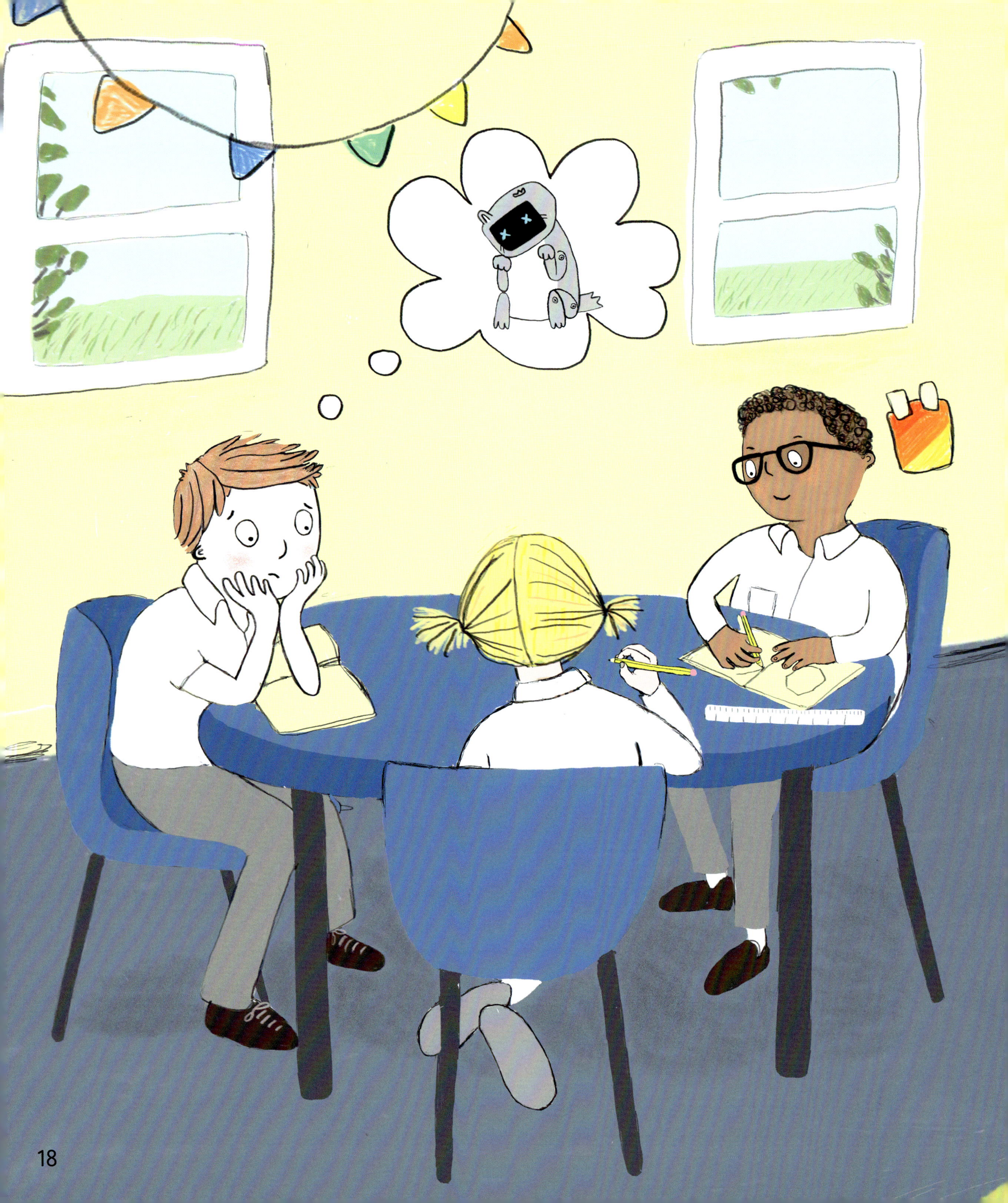

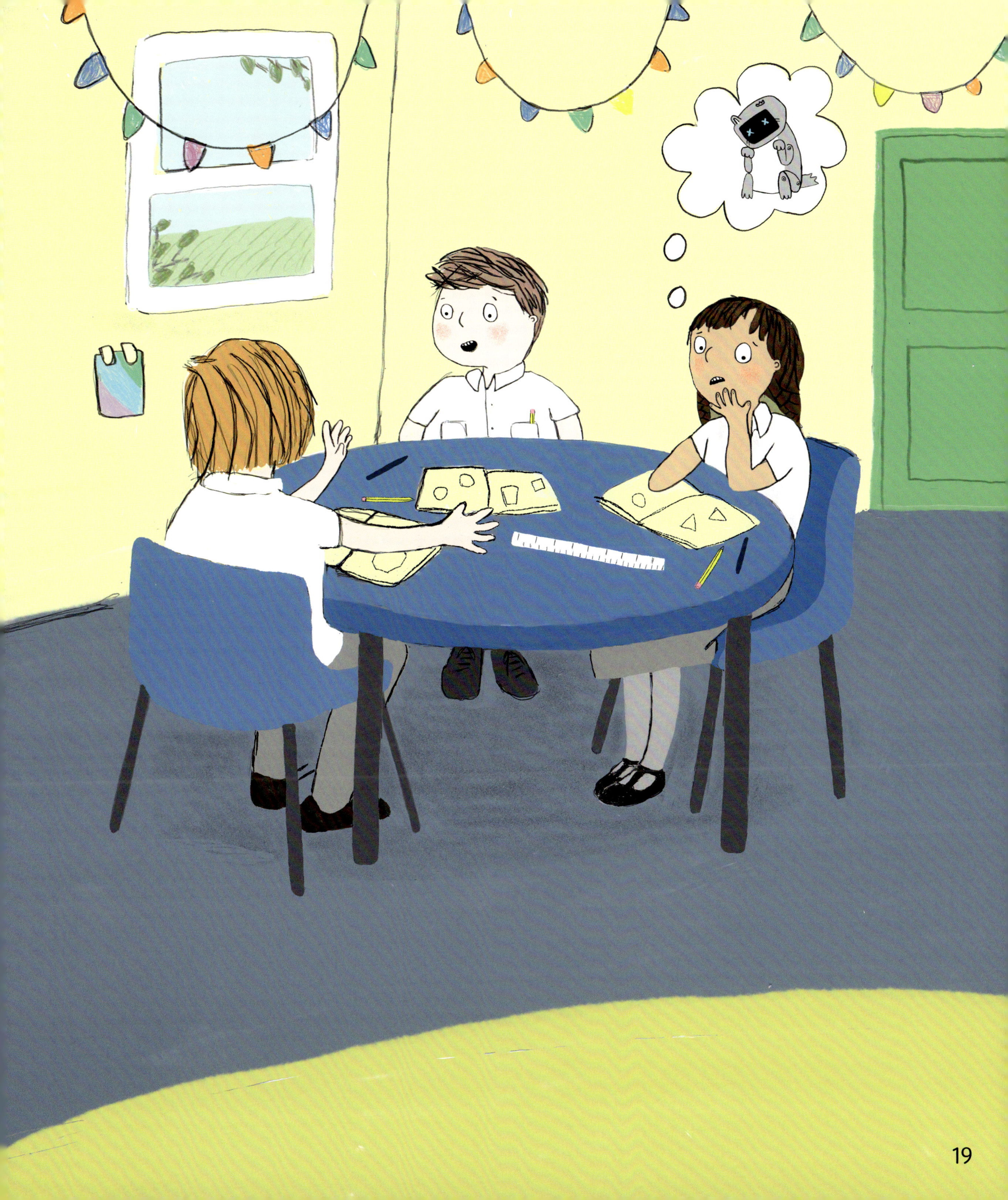

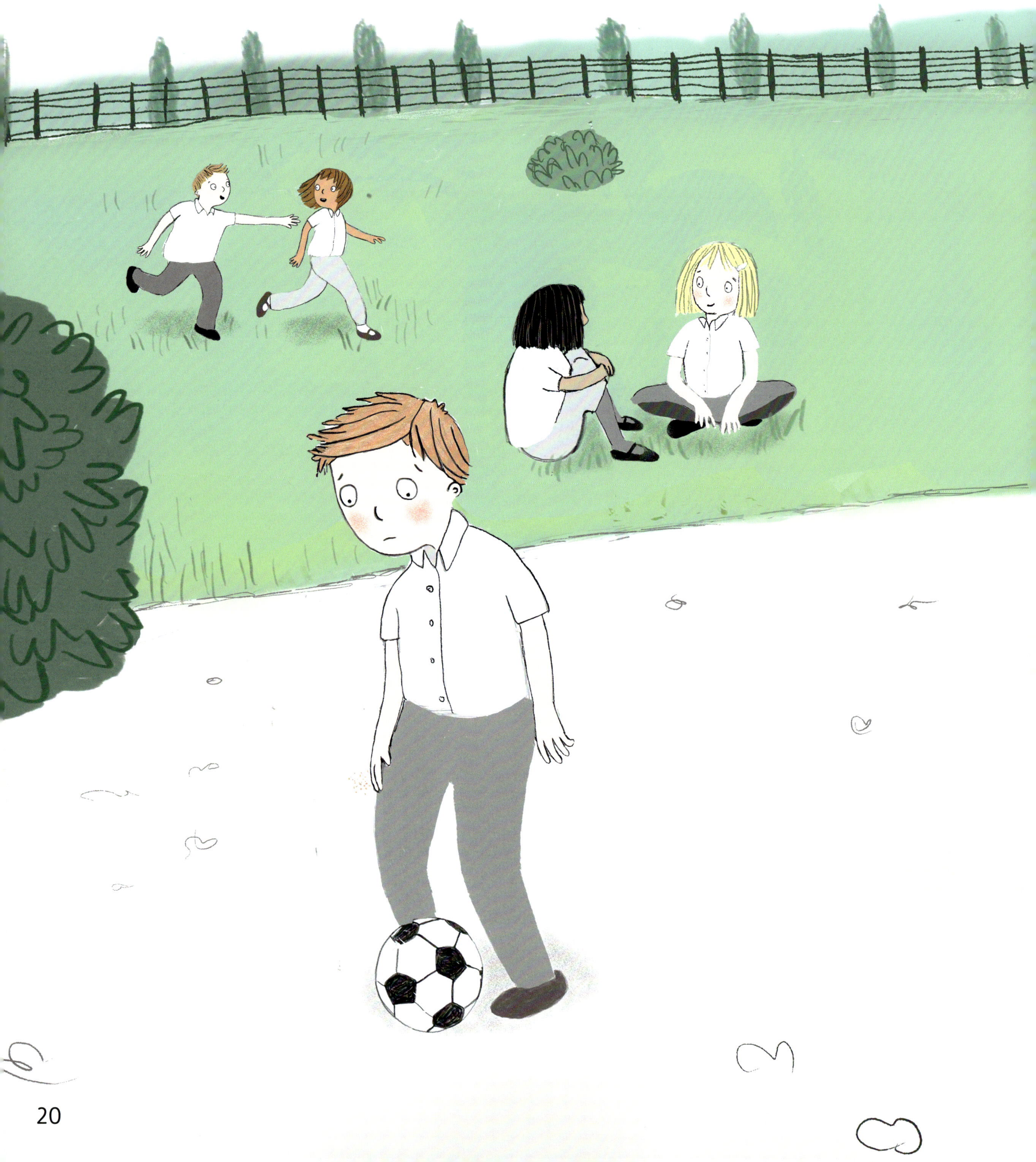

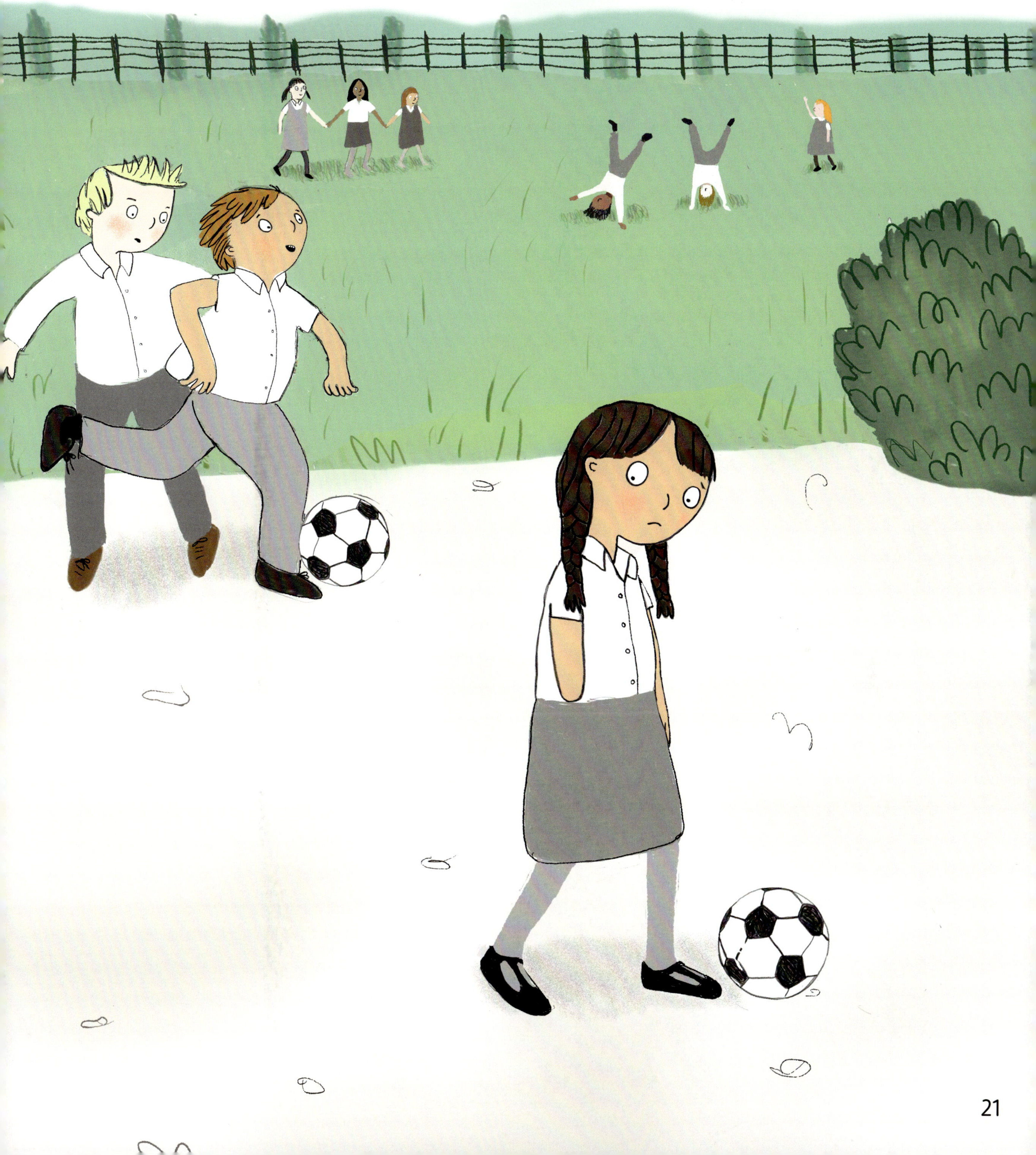

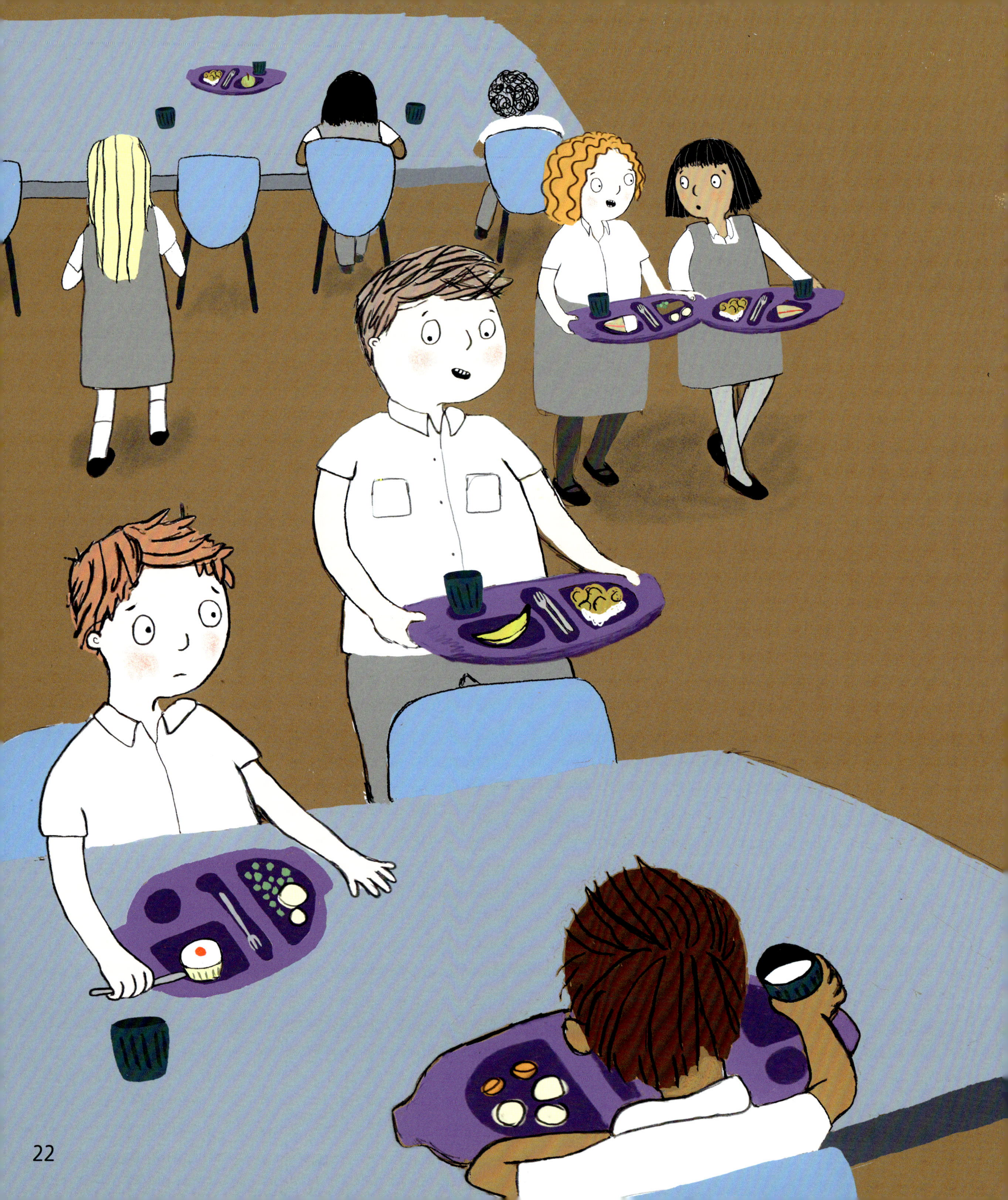

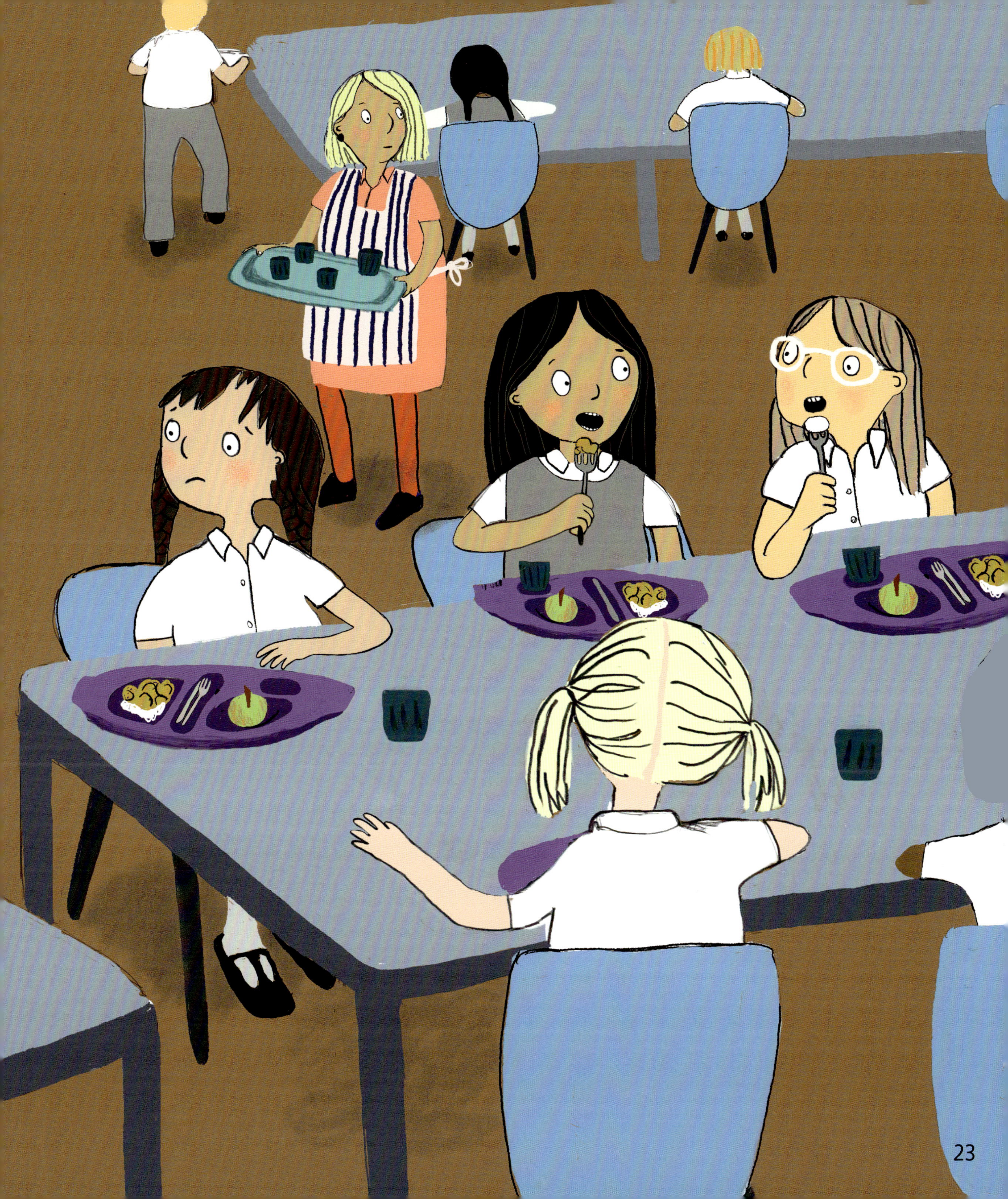

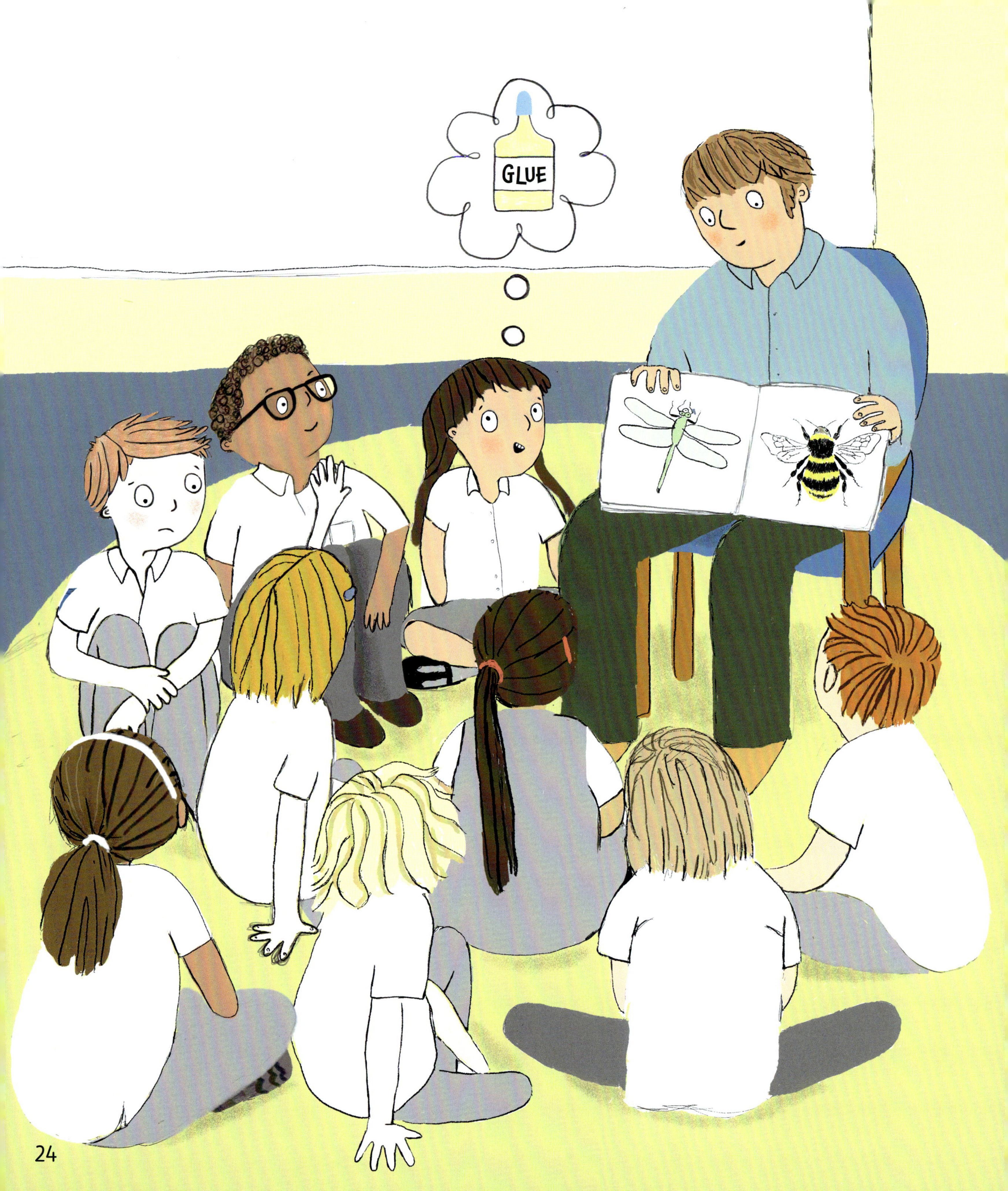
GLUE

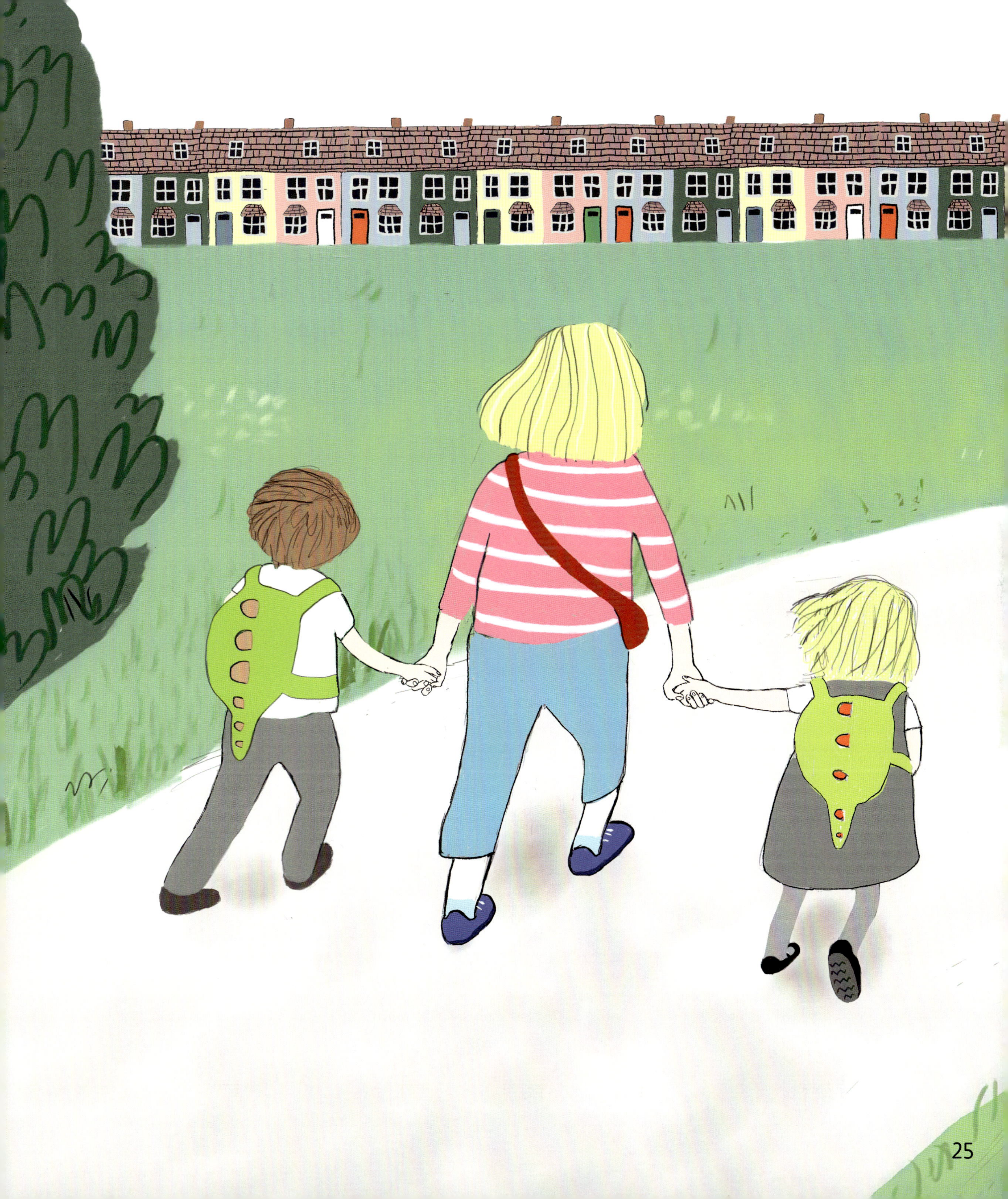

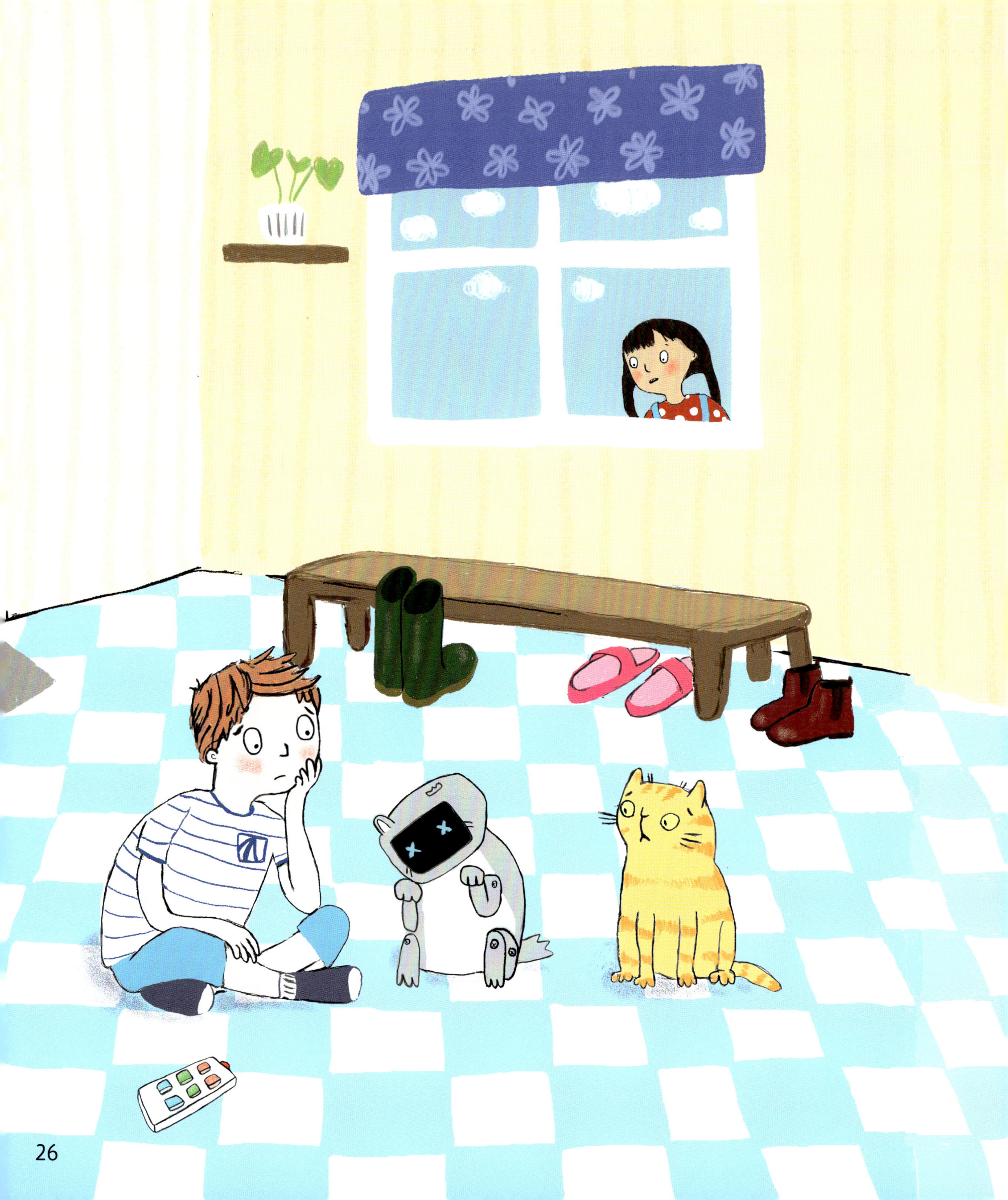

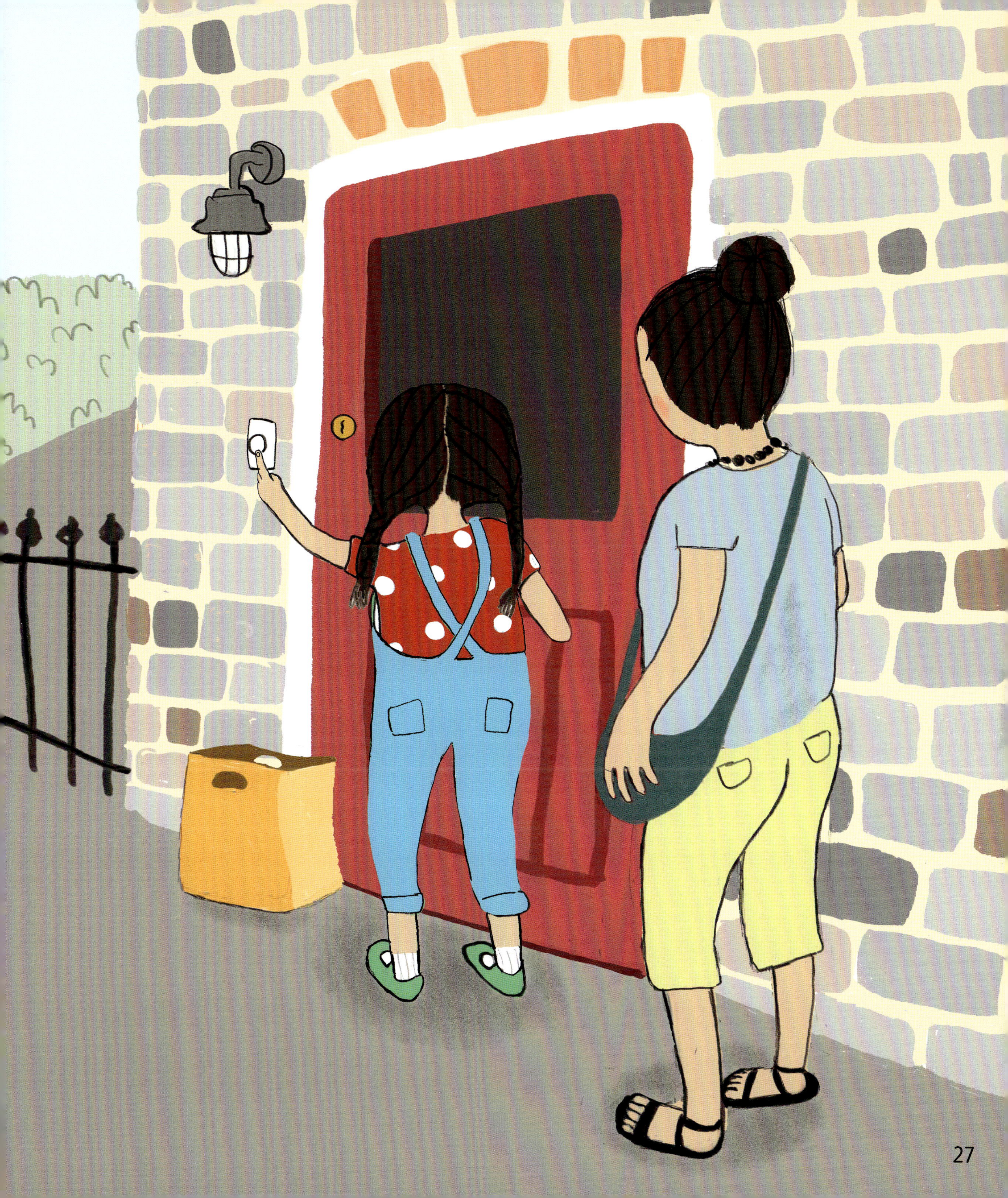

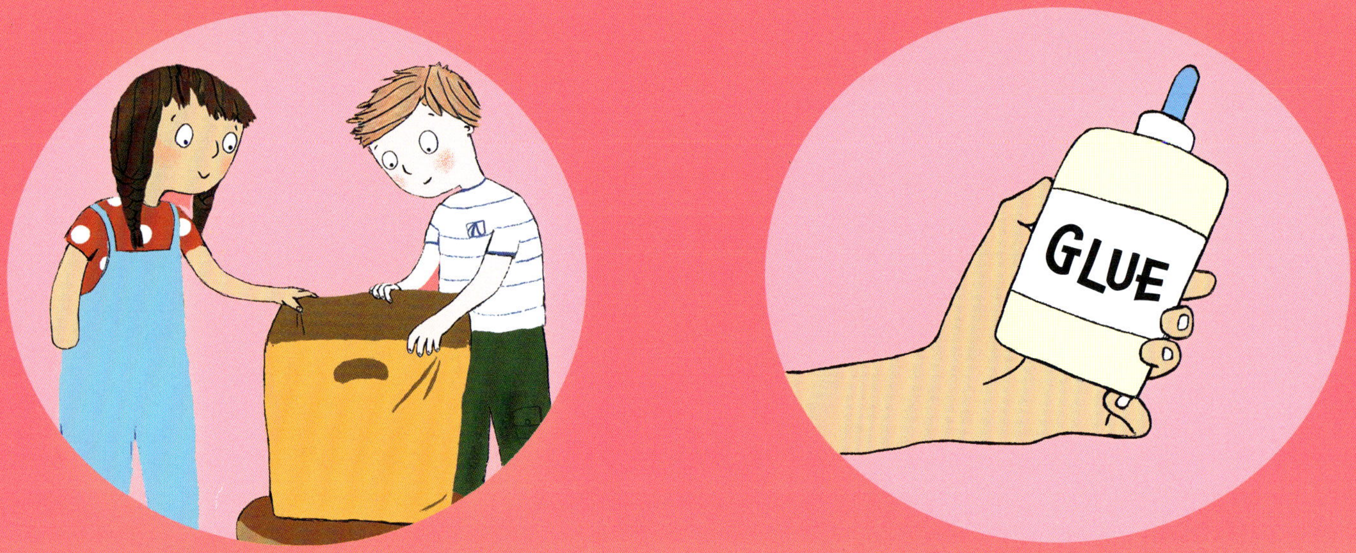
GLUE
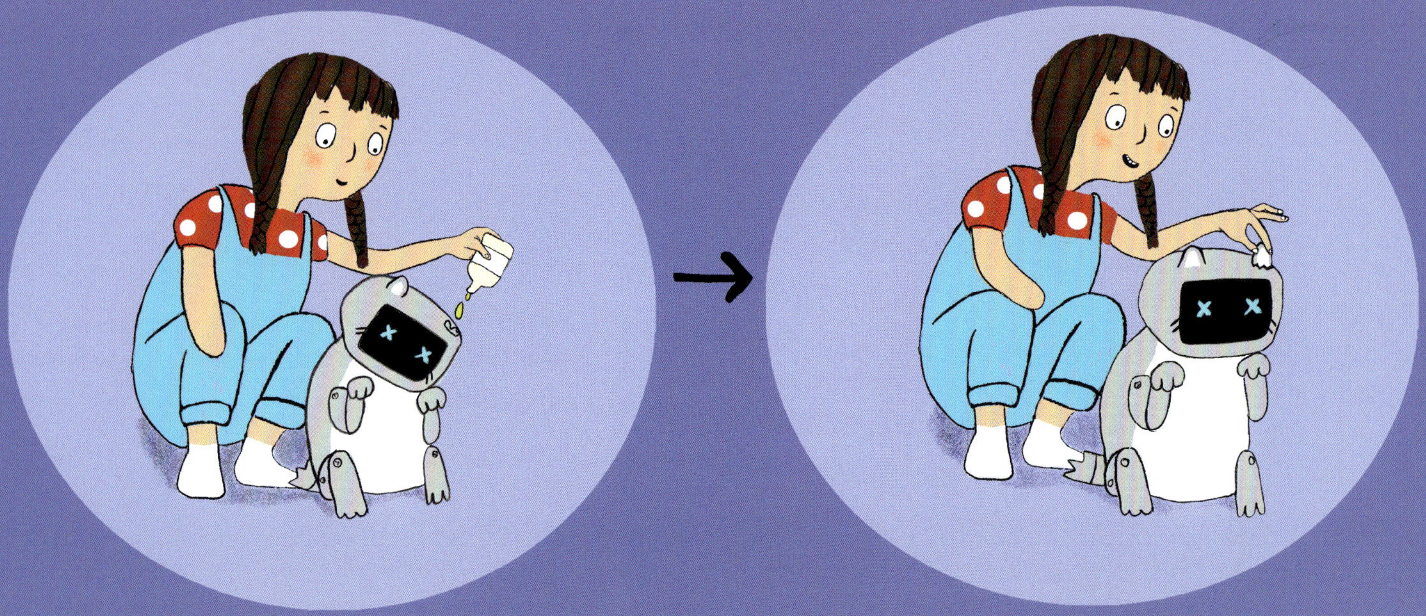
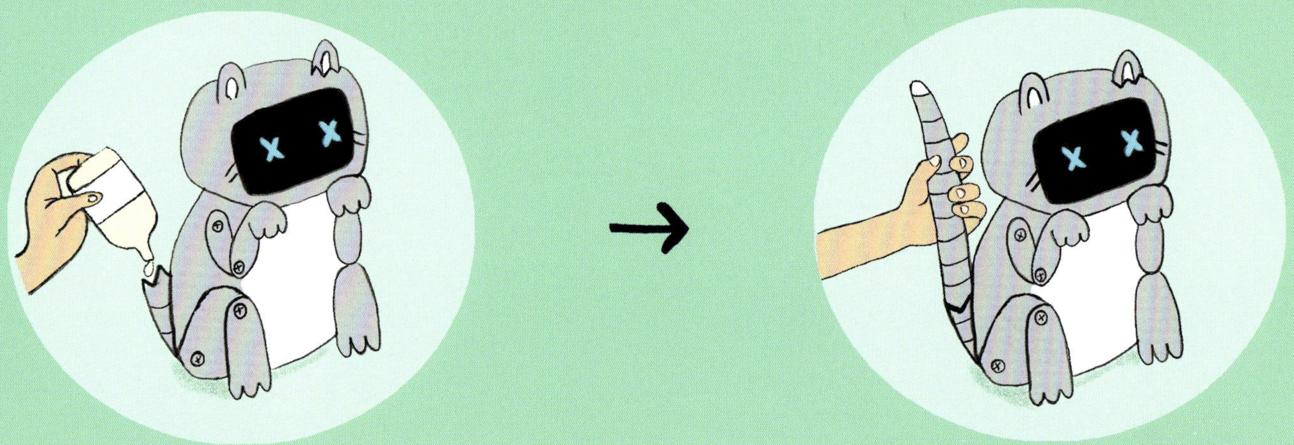

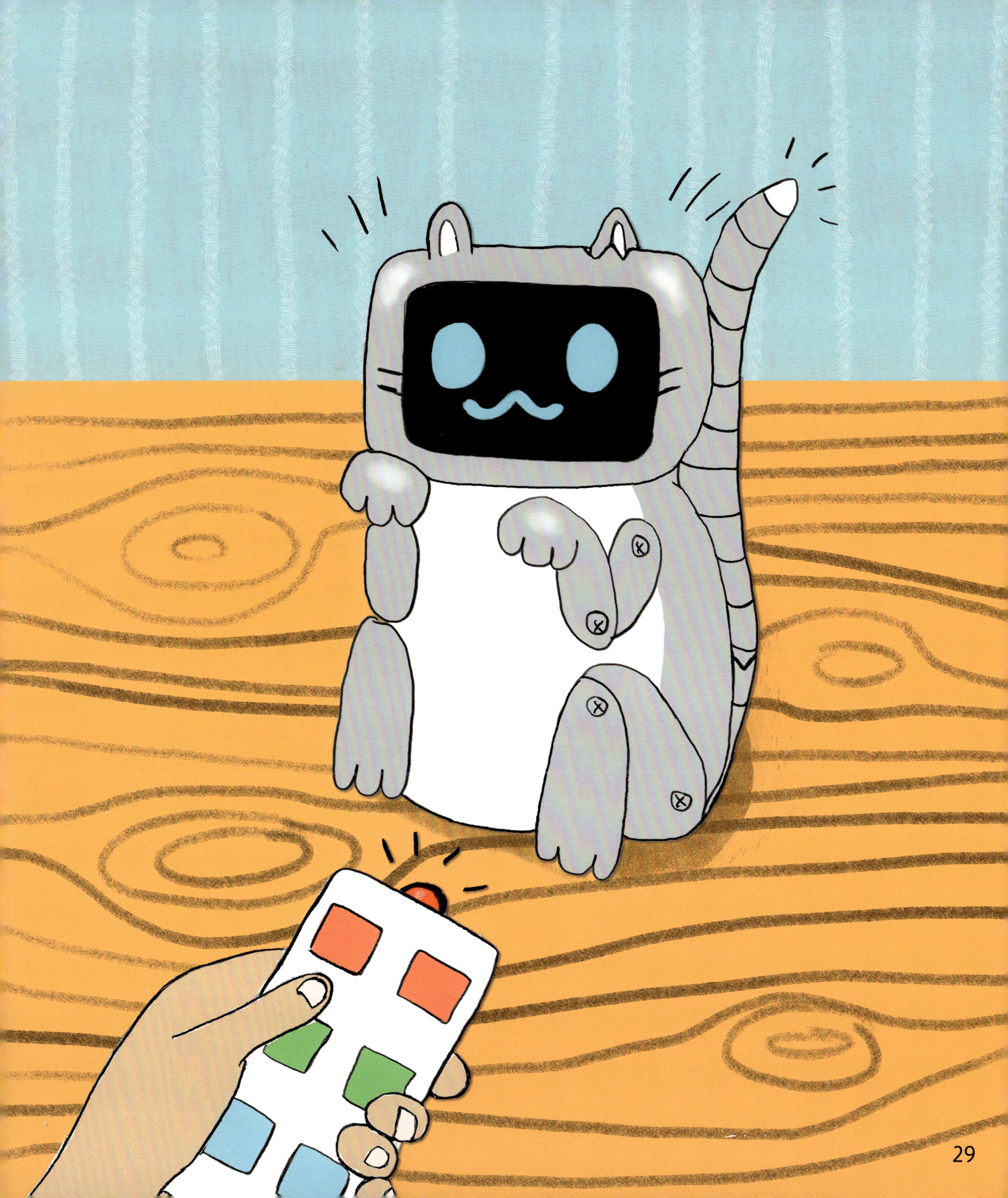

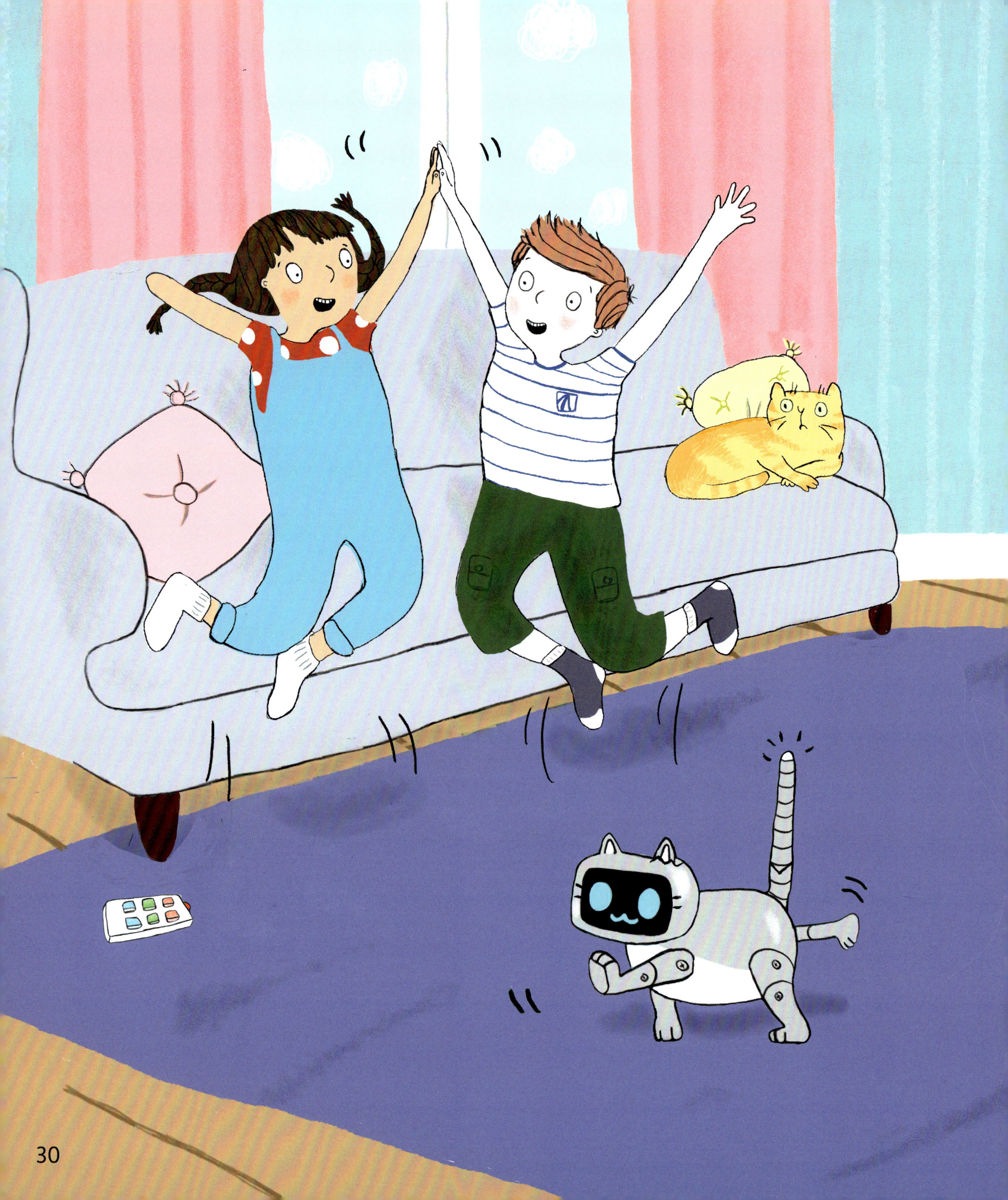

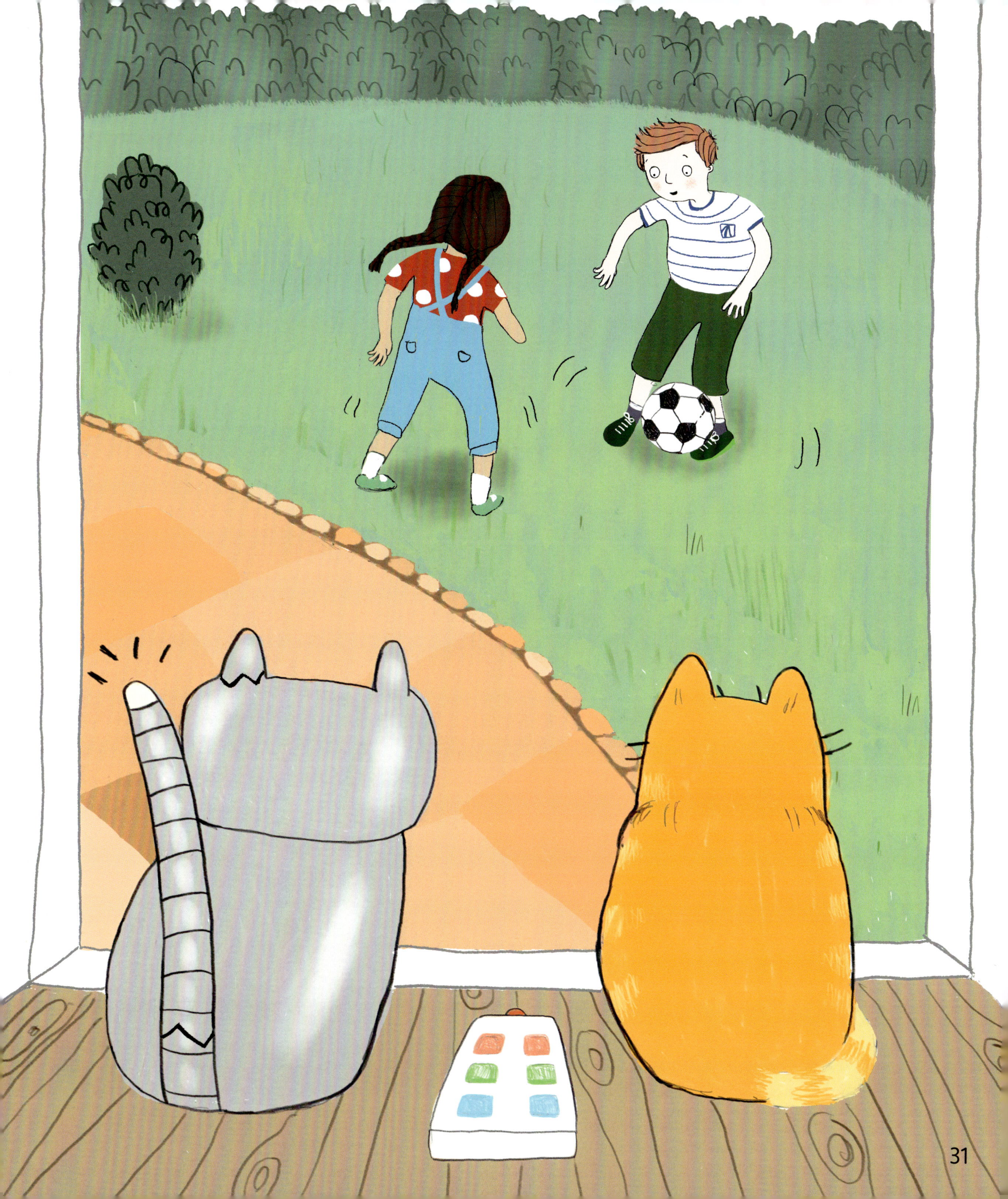

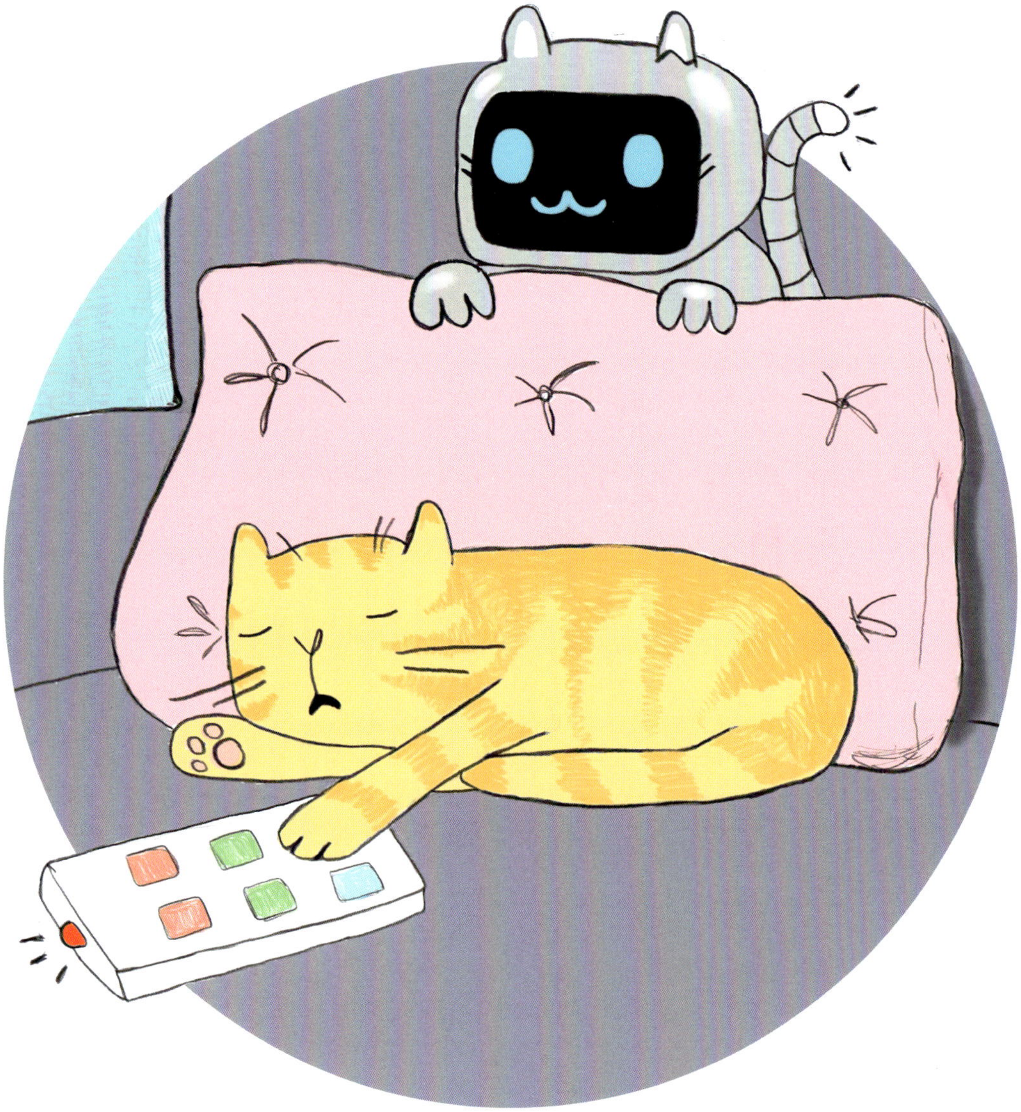